How to Manage Your Money Workbook

HOW TO MANAGE YOUR MONEY WORKBOOK

LARRY BURKETT

Moody Press
Chicago

ISBN: 0-8024-1476-1

1 3 5 7 9 10 8 6 4 2

Printed in the United States of America

HOW TO MANAGE YOUR MONEY WORKBOOK

Contents

Introduction

Chapter

INTRODUCTION

Welcome to *How to Manage Your Money*. In the 1970s, when the ministry of Christian Financial Concepts began, there was not a lot of study material focusing on how believers could serve God through the responsible use of money. It seemed that stewardship was discussed most often on Missions Sunday or when the church introduced its new building program to the congregation. So, there was a lot of interest in my early seminars when I shared what the Bible says about the everyday aspects of money, poverty, and wealth. There is so much religious folklore in the financial realm that few Christians understand what is from God's Word and what is not.

Now that I have taught this subject for many years—in Bible studies, on radio and television, through cassette tapes, CDs, and videos—I know what a revelation it is for most Christians to discover how much God cares about money.

There are about 700 direct references to money in the Bible, along with hundreds more indirect references. Nearly two-thirds of Jesus' parables deal with the use of money. He equated the ability to manage financial resources with the ability to manage spiritual resources.

> *"He who is faithful in a very little thing is faithful also in much; and he who is unrighteous in a very little thing is unrighteous also in much. Therefore if you have not been faithful in the use of unrighteous wealth, who will entrust the true riches to you?"* (Luke 16:10-11).

My hope is that, as a result of this study, you will gain absolute peace from the Lord in the area of finances, because that's what God promises in His Word. Don't wait until you have completed the entire study to apply God's principles. As you recognize a need in your life, apply God's Word. Share these principles with others and discuss them freely. God wants His truth to shape your situation, rather than your situation to shape God's truth.

For too long, Christians have pretended that they have no financial problems, which of course is nonsense. The truth is that finances are major "war zones" in our battle against Satan. We are subject to the same attacks and temptations as nonbelievers. It is only through obedience to God's Word and His blessing that we can escape those attacks. But how can we experience God's blessing if we don't understand His plan? We can't, so this study will focus exclusively on understanding God's principles of finance.

Remember, these are God's *principles*—not His laws. He doesn't threaten to punish those who violate these principles; however, those who do violate them, and struggle with the consequences, will not be able to receive His blessings in the area of finances. Most of the rewards promised in Scripture are predicated on our obedience to these principles. Therefore, to receive these rewards, we must be able to understand and follow God's plan.

Perhaps your financial life is in order and you are experiencing God's blessings in your day-to-day life. But maybe you've never understood the scriptural basis for doing what you have done. If this is your situation, you will enjoy this study, because it will enable you to transfer your knowledge and experience to others. You can share these concepts and their application on a biblically sound basis.

How to Use This Study

Although you can complete this workbook on your own, the material is designed to be used in group discussions whenever possible. The scriptural principles are presented from God's Word, and writing space is provided for individual participation and application. Read the Scriptures, write your own analysis, and prepare to share your insights with others in your group. There is no time requirement for each session. Proceed as quickly or as slowly as the group decides, but stick to a regular schedule (such as one session per week). By using this method, the study will fit most church-based Sunday school schedules. Many study areas are thought-provoking and controversial, and if you tie up an entire study session on one issue, it will be difficult to finish the entire plan. It is often preferable to prepare and evaluate a section before opening the discussion to questions.

To encourage you, at the end of each chapter we have included unedited testimonials that were shared with Christian Financial Concepts by people like you.

WHAT IS WEALTH?

"Instruct them to do good, to be rich in good works, to be generous and ready to share, storing up for themselves the treasure of a good foundation for the future, so that they may take hold of that which is life indeed" (1 Timothy 6:18-19).

WHAT IS WEALTH?

God's Definition of Wealth

When you hear someone talk about wealth, what images come to your mind? stacks of money? luxury vehicles? a yacht? a mansion? diamonds and furs? world travel?

Do you work to earn the money you and your family need? And does it seem that no matter how hard you work you can't generate enough money to satisfy all of your family's wants and desires? So, what is wealth? And how does one acquire it?

Historically, wealth has been related to ownership of tangible assets–things people could see and touch: land, camels, cattle, or slaves. This has been true since Bible times.

Currently, wealth often is expressed in intangible assets. For example, we talk in terms of how many dollars an individual is worth. A dollar doesn't have an objective value as an item; it has an intangible value—you can't eat it or wear it. Similarly, the value of a stock is not based on the value of the company; it's based on its investors' collective opinion about the stock. Even gold, which has served as a measure of wealth through the ages, is based on opinion, as illustrated by sharp speculative increases and decreases.

Wealth also is related to your creative ability: the value people place on your performance—for example, professional athletes. Then there is your credit or borrowing ability: the trust others have in you. So, wealth becomes a factor in your identity, your perceived value, and your trustworthiness.

Depending on the balance in these areas, wealth can be used for good (spreading the Gospel and furthering God's kingdom) or bad (bribing officials or building bombs). Wealth represents power, so it is not unusual that most people want as much of it as they can get.

Neither our abundance nor our lack of money affects our relationship with Him, but our attitudes do.

What Is Wealth?

In the past, opportunities for acquiring wealth were limited. However, in our own lifetime there has been an amazing shift in the ways wealth can be accumulated. Most of the wealthy people in the U.S. today did not become wealthy by inheritance. For example, the wealthiest man in America is Bill Gates, founder of Microsoft. He made his fortune by creating a company that sells ideas, rather than tangible products.

On the surface, it seems that the rules of wealth have changed. Stock market booms create overnight millionaires. State lotteries make a few winners instantly rich. The Internet makes millionaires of young people who look like they should be cutting grass for pocket change.

And here you are, working hard, even struggling to get ahead in a financial world that seems to be passing you by. Why should it be so hard for you when financial success seems to come so easily to others?

Clearly, for God's people wealth should mean more than just the accumulation of material possessions. If wealth alone brought happiness, the wealthiest people should be the happiest. Evidence shows that the exact opposite is often true. God's plan is that we should have true wealth.

> *"It is the blessing of the Lord that makes rich, and He adds no sorrow to it"* (**Proverbs 10:22**).

What does this verse mean to you? *If a blessing is of the Lord it should cause no sorrow.*

Study Questions

1. What is the basic difference between the resources supplied by God and those delivered by the world?

   God promises *all we need*

   The world usually delivers *only things that bring sorrow*

   What difference should there be in a Christian's material life?

   Seek the things of God

"Do not store up for yourselves treasures on earth, where moth and rust destroy, and where thieves break in and steal. But store up for yourselves treasures in heaven, where neither moth nor rust destroys, and where thieves do not break in or steal" (Matthew 6:19–20).

2. Does this mean Christians should never save? _____ yes __✓__ no

   Explain *Yes, but more like Joseph did for the Egyptians, not excessively.*

3. Should we give away all our surplus? _____ yes __✓__ no

   but most of it.

4. How does the following verse relate?

   "How blessed is the [one] *who finds wisdom and the* [one] *who gains understanding. For her profit is better than the profit of silver and her gain better than fine gold"* (Proverbs 3:13-14).

   That to gain wisdom and understanding (esp. about Christ) is better than any wealth.

The Christian's Wealth

God is concerned with our attitudes about money and possessions. Neither our abundance nor our lack of money affects our relationship with Him, but our attitudes do. We are not reflecting His character when we are angry or depressed because of our financial situations.

As Christians, we must learn how to trust God in every circumstance and believe that He loves us and that He will give us what we can handle without being tempted beyond what we can withstand. How we use material resources is a testing ground that reveals our true priorities.

Wealth is neither moral nor immoral. It is not God's design for His people to live in poverty. There is no inherent virtue in poverty. There are dishonest poor as well as rich, and there are honorable rich as well as poor. God opposes the misuse of or the preoccupation with wealth–not wealth itself.

In fact, Romans 12 lists the gift of giving as a spiritual gift. Having the ability to develop resources and produce financially is implied in exercising this gift.

"We, who are many, are one body in Christ, and individually members one of another. Since we have gifts that differ according to the grace given to us, each

How we use material resources is a testing ground that reveals out true priorities.

Attitude

of us is to exercise them accordingly…He who gives, with liberality" (Romans
12:5-6,8).

Study Questions

1. What does God say about money and happiness? Summarize what the following
    verses say about them.

    a. *"Instruct those who are rich in this present world not to be conceited or to fix
        their hope on the uncertainty of riches, but on God, who richly supplies us
        with all things to enjoy"* (1 Timothy 6:17).

        Depend on God, not on our
        selves and our money

    b. *"Riches do not profit in the day of wrath, but righteousness delivers from
        death"* (Proverbs 11:4).

        When we die it will not
        matter what wealth we have,
        but being declared righteous by
        Christ will save you from death

2. Is having wealth a sin? Write one pertinent point from each of the following verses.

    a. *"There is precious treasure and oil in the dwelling of the wise, but a foolish
        man swallows it up"* (Proverbs 21:20).

        The foolish spend all they get.

    b. *"The reward of humility and the fear of the Lord are riches, honor and life"*
        (Proverbs 22:4).

        You are rich if you know
        Jesus and humble yourself to Him.

3. What attitude does God expect from us? Give a brief analysis of each verse.

a. *"So you will find favor and good repute in the sight of God and man. Trust in the Lord will all your heart and do not lean on your own understanding. In all your ways acknowledge Him, and He will make your paths straight"* (Proverbs 3:4–6).

   Constantly check with God and do what He asks and you will have (straight paths?)

b. *"Long life is in her [Wisdom's] right hand; in her left hand are riches and honor. Her ways are pleasant ways, and all her paths are peace"* (Proverbs 3:16–17).

   More peace in life if wise

4. Realistically, what can we expect from God? Give your answers below.

a. *"Riches and honor are with me [Wisdom], enduring wealth and righteousness"* (Proverbs 8:18).

   blessed by God if you're wise

b. *"By me [Wisdom] your days will be multiplied, and years of life will be added to you"* (Proverbs 9:11).

   Live longer if your wise

5. In four words, what is the real danger of wealth?

   a. "*The love of money is a root of all sorts of evil, and some by longing for it have wandered away from the faith and pierced themselves with many griefs*" (1 Timothy 6:10).

   leads us away from God

   b. "*Jesus said to His disciples, 'Truly I say to you, it is hard for a rich man to enter the kingdom of heaven. Again I say to you, it is easier for a camel to go through the eye of a needle, than for a rich man to enter the kingdom of God.' When the disciples heard this, they were very astonished and said, 'Then who can be saved?' And looking at them Jesus said to them, 'With people this is impossible, but with God all things are possible'* " (Matthew 19:23–26).

   The man's real problem was *trying to save himself or buy his way to heaven*

Living Proof Testimony

A female prison inmate writes, expressing a practical understanding of God's definition of wealth through her actions, attitude, and desire to encourage others.

"*Even on a state [correctional] inmate wages of 45 cents an hour, I made a budget and stick to it. I pay my tithe faithfully (10%), pay on my courts costs and restitution (my debts, 20%), and save (10%). I've paid off several of my debts, have saved $200, and send some money home to my son.*

"*I feel most blessed. I encourage anyone, no matter what their income (mine's $72 a month) to give God control of their finances. They'll never regret it. God bless you.*"

GOD'S WILL IN FINANCES

"In Him all the fullness of Diety dwells in bodily form, and in Him you have been made complete, and He is the head over all rule and authority" (Colossians 2:9-10).

GOD'S WILL IN FINANCES

Stewardship

The key to understanding God's will in finances is the proper understanding of stewardship. Webster's dictionary says that a steward is a person who manages another's property. We are merely stewards of God's property. He can choose to entrust us to manage as much or as little as He desires, but in no case will we ever become owners.

In Genesis, the Bible presents one view of the material world: It all belongs to God. The Garden of Eden was God's; Adam and Eve merely tended it. God gave them permission to enjoy the garden as their own, with one restriction. When they violated that one restriction, they were evicted.

Then in the Psalms, David wrote that *"The earth is the Lord's, and all it contains, the world, and those who dwell in it"* (Psalm 24:1).

If as Christians we can accept our role as stewards and manage God's resources according to His direction, He will entrust us with even more. But why would He entrust more of His property to us if we hoard and act like owners? When we acknowledge God's total ownership, we can experience God's miraculous and wise direction in all areas of responsibility, including financial management. Although properly managing all areas of life is important to God, this book focuses on the management of money. Let's explore what God's Word says about it.

In Matthew we read "The Parable of the Talents," but we should call it "The Parable of the Steward," because that is its focus. When Jesus told this story, a talent was known as a unit of money. (Before that time, it was a unit of weight.) Today, many think of this story in terms of all of our resources, gifts, and abilities.

His plans for us are not always the same as our desires.

Study Questions

1. Read Matthew 25:14-30 and answer the following questions.

    a. To what did Christ equate this parable?

    Kingdom of Heaven

    b. Why was each given a different amount?

    in proportion to their abilities

    c. Did the owner ask or expect each to earn exactly the same?

    No because they were given different amounts.

    d. How were the two faithful servants rewarded?

    praised and given more responsibilities

    e. What happened to the last servant?

    thrown to outer darkness

    The key theme in this parable is *stewardship*. We are to use our abilities, manage the Master's resources well, and then return them to Him.

2. Compare "The Parable of the Steward" with that found in Luke 12:16–20. It is called by some "The Parable of the Rich Fool."

    a. How is this farmer described? _rich, very productive (proud, greedy)_

    b. Did God object to his wealth?

    no his atitude

    c. Where did the farmer go wrong?

    believing he did not need to consult God

    d. Why did God rebuke him?

    He was only seeing wealth as his Savior, not God.

3. Read Luke 12:25-34 and describe the elements of becoming God's steward.

   a. How does God assess our abilities as owners? (verses 25-26)

   Not able to do anything, but afraid of all things

   b. What is God's promise? (verses 27, 31)

   Promises to cloth and give necessarities

   c. What should our attitude be? (verse 32)

   Not to fear God gives us heaven

   d. What does God ask of us? (verse 33)

   Invest in heaven

   e. Why? (verse 34)

   For where your treasure is, there will your heart also be.

How God Uses Finances

Often God uses money in our lives as a means of direction, because it is an area in which most of us are sensitive and vulnerable. If we are open to it, He promises to supply His wisdom and direction. But His plans for us are not always the same as our desires. So, we must be willing to accept His plan.

We may be tempted to strike out on our own path without clear direction from God and then expect Him to make everything work out for us. In effect, that is asking Him to bless our priorities and plans over His own. We need to look for God's guidance signals, including His "STOP" and "YIELD" commands. In some countries, the yield sign reads "GIVE WAY." This is what God wants us to do as He reveals His will.

When we fail to yield, we have decided that our wisdom is superior to His. It never is, and learning this lesson sometimes can be costly. The price we eventually pay for going our own way can be money, time, and, most assuredly, peace!

This study will help you understand the irrefutable wisdom of handling money God's way.

start

Study Questions

1. Trust

In the following verses, God makes a promise to us as His children.

   "For the Gentiles eagerly seek all these things; for your heavenly Father knows that you need all these things. But seek first His kingdom and His righteousness, and all these things will be added to you" (Matthew 6:32-33).

   What is His promise?

   given all we need

   What is His prerequisite? _seek first His kingdom and His righteousness._

2. Ability to Supply

   "Therefore I say to you, all things for which you pray and ask, believe that you have received them, and they will be granted you" (Mark 11:24).

   What can we trust God for if we are truly in His will? _all things for which you pray._

3. Trustworthiness

   "Therefore if you have not been faithful in the use of unrighteous wealth, who will entrust the true riches to you?" (Luke 16:11).

   God expects certain minimum responses from us. In this verse, God equates _money_ to _heaven_ .

4. Love

   Sometimes, Christians fail to trust God because they believe inwardly that He wants to punish and deprive them. What does the following verse promise?

   "If you then, being evil, know how to give good gifts to your children, how much more will your Father who is in heaven give what is good to those who ask Him!" (Matthew 7:11).

   that God wants to give good gifts to those who ask Him

   Remember, God _loves_ us.

5. God Wants to Show That He Does What He Says

In writing to many early Christians who did not know much about the God of the Bible, the apostle Paul quoted the following Old Testament promise, which is also true today.

> *"The Scripture says, 'Whoever believes in Him will not be disappointed.' For there is no distinction between Jew and Greek; for the same Lord is Lord of all, abounding in riches for all who call upon Him"* (**Romans 10:11–12**).

a. Whoever _believes_ will not be disappointed.

b. God does not _discriminate, but gives to all who call upon Him._

The key word here is *believe*.

SESSION 2

One of the most important characteristics of the Christian life and commitment is patience.

6. Unification

God uses material possessions to unify the body of Christ. Here is a two-part lesson.

> *"This is not for the ease of others and for your affliction, but by way of equality—at this present time your abundance being a supply for their need, so that their abundance also may become a supply for your need, that there may be equality"* (**2 Corinthians 8:13-14**).

a. What do we share from? _our abundance_

b. Why? _to make things equal – supply another's need_

The following verse describes God's plan for our surpluses in His economic order.

> *"As it is written, 'He who gathered much did not have too much, and he who gathered little had no lack'"* (**2 Corinthians 8:15**).

The apostle Paul describes God's plan for our surpluses: If we have too much and others have too little, it results in _sharing our surplus_.

7. Direction

One of the most important characteristics of the Christian life and commitment is patience. It is virtually impossible to be obedient and impatient at the same time. God will use resources (money) as a means of revealing our obedience to His will rather than our own.

> *"Trust in the Lord with all your heart, and do not lean on your own understanding. In all your ways acknowledge Him, and He will make your paths straight"* (**Proverbs 3:5–6**).

Complete the principles from these verses.

a. Trust in _the Lord with all your heart_.

b. Do not lean on _your own understanding_

c. Then He will _make your paths straight_
(give you direction)

*"Let us not lose heart in doing good, for in due time we will reap if we do not
grow weary"* (**Galatians 6:9**).

What is this verse's main message? _continue to give_
to God's work and He will bless
us in His time.

8. Witness

One of the most effective witnesses to many non-Christians is presented in the use
of money. It is one thing to say you love others, but how do you show that love?
The following verse is from the Old Testament.

> *"The poor will never cease to be in the land; therefore I command you, saying,
> 'You shall freely open your hand to your brother, to your needy and poor in your
> land'"* (**Deuteronomy 15:11**).

According to this verse, what does God command us to do?

give to the needy and poor

> *"Truly I say to you, to the extent that you did not do it to one of the least of
> these, you did not do it to Me"* (**Matthew 25:45**).

In the New Testament, God equates helping the truly needy with _~~not~~_
giving to God.

Living Proof Testimony

A first-time *Money Matters* budgeting software user tells how she and her husband view their financial responsibilities as stewards of God.

"You are right, Larry, it [Money Matters] *is easy to use. I am caught up with our records now and will soon teach my husband how it works. My husband is a disabled veteran and suffering with multiple sclerosis. Because of his difficulty he allows me to manage our finances, but we both decide how we spend or save our money.*

"The guiding principle that we try to follow is that it is the Lord's money entrusted to us and we are His stewards. We thank the Lord for all His blessings and faithfulness in our lives."

SESSION 2

THE PERILS OF MONEY

"Make sure that your character is free from the love of money, being content with what you have; for He Himself has said, 'I will never desert you, nor will I ever forsake you'" (Hebrews 13:5).

THE PERILS OF MONEY

Servitude to Money

→ Just as God can use money to enhance and direct our lives, Satan can use it to shackle us and get us off course. Christians should learn to recognize the danger of money entanglements and financial bondage.

Until recent times, financial bondage also meant physical bondage. If debtors couldn't pay what they owed, they were thrown into debtors' prison. In Scripture we see this practice described.

make friends of the people you owe so they will not take you to jail for what you owe.

"Make friends quickly with your opponent at law while you are with him on the way, so that your opponent may not hand you over to the judge, and the judge to the officer, and you be thrown into prison. Truly I say to you, you will not come out of there until you have paid up the last cent" (Matthew 5:25–26).

Debtors' prisons no longer exist in our country, but they have been replaced by something that is equally bad: worry or mental bondage. Each year millions of marriages are destroyed by financial worries caused by the financial pressures of debt and poor money management (financial bondage). Why? Because the couples have violated one or more biblical principles in the way they handle money.

It's not simply the lack of money that results in bondage. In the New Testament, God shows that His expectation for us to help the poor is still in place.

Often an abundance results in mental anguish. If there is too little money, people worry about gaining more; and, if there is too much, they worry about losing it. Attitude is the key, as seen in God's Word.

Attitude is the key, as seen in God's Word.

The Bible does not prohibit borrowing or lending, but it warns of problems that can accompany being on either side of debt.

Our integrity and witness as Christians obligates us to repay what we owe.

Too many times we treat symptoms rather than problems.

Study Questions

1. Attitude

   Two principles are discussed in these verses.

   > *"Two things I asked of You, do not refuse me before I die: keep deception and lies far from me, give me neither poverty nor riches; feed me with the food that is my portion, that I not be full and deny You and say, 'Who is the Lord?' Or that I not be in want and steal, and profane the name of my God"* **(Proverbs 30:7–9).**

   a. The danger of riches is ___*deny God*___

   b. The danger of poverty is ___*stealing and profaning name of God*___

   The principle is clear when dealing with poverty (honesty versus dishonesty). But the distinction is not as clear with wealth. Why? Because we become content without God.

2. God's Attitude Toward Debt

   There is much confusion regarding whether a Christian should borrow money. The Bible does not prohibit borrowing or lending, but it warns of problems that can accompany being on either side of debt. God does not want us to be in bondage, because it inhibits our ability to serve Him.

   Debts are delinquent financial obligations. If we borrow money and repay it according to agreement, we are not "in debt" in the context of this discussion; it is a financial obligation (i.e., a loan). But when we fail to honor an agreement, we are in debt. To avoid bondage to the lender, we need to repay our financial obligations quickly and responsibly.

3. Bondage Through Debt

   One of the most common causes of bondage is the abuse of credit.

   > *"The rich rules over the poor, and the borrower becomes the lender's slave"* **(Proverbs 22:7).**

   This principle should make us cautious about borrowing. When people consciously borrow beyond their normal ability to repay, usually it is because they lack the self-discipline or the strength of character to deny themselves what they can't afford.

   Then what do the borrowers become? ___*lender's slave*___

4. Indulgence

It's easy to rationalize an indulgent lifestyle in a society in which the majority of people indulge themselves. People who are never willing to sacrifice or deny impulses to spend will always be in financial bondage.

God speaks to the attitude, not to the act. Most debt is the result of an unscriptural attitude.

> *"Like a city that is broken into and without walls is a man who has no control over his spirit"* (Proverbs 25:28).

What should we beware of? *our attitude*

There are two Scripture verses that relate to this principle. Read Proverbs 16:18 and 21:20. *16:18 Pride goes before destruction, a haughty spirit before a fall. 21:20 In the house of the wise are stores of choice food & oil, but a foolish man devours all he has.*

5. Avoiding Debt

Is bankruptcy scriptural? It seems logical that if someone has incurred excessive debts and has a truly changed attitude, that person should be able to start afresh, doesn't it?

> *"The wicked borrows and does not pay back, but the righteous is gracious and gives"* (Psalm 37:21).

God says that one who borrows and does not repay is *wicked*

Sometimes, legal relief is sought to protect others to whom debts are owed, but the principle is that even if the law relieves the financial obligations, our integrity and witness as Christians obligates us to repay what we owe.

God's Word refers to the use of credit in this principle:

> *"If you have not been faithful in the use of that which is another's, who will give you that which is your own?"* (Luke 16:12).

Describe this principle of credit in your own words. *If you do not use wisely the money loaned you and repay in a timely fashion — you may not have anything.* "own"

The Bible does not prohibit borrowing or lending, but it warns of problems that can accompany being on either side of debt.

Is God's plan logical? Probably not. In worldly terms, to avoid debtors seems more logical. A common response of the borrower is, "How will I ever pay back all this debt?" God's Word has the answer.

"Offer to God a sacrifice of thanksgiving and pay your vows to the Most High; call upon Me in the day of trouble; I shall rescue you, and you will honor Me" **(Psalm 50:14–15).**

If we _call_ Him, God promises to _rescue us_ .

When Christians transfer assets simply to avoid creditors, it reflects a basic lack of trust and a deceitful attitude.

God always looks into our hearts. As we read in Genesis 22:1–18, when God asked Abraham to sacrifice his son Isaac, which to Abraham represented everything, God looked into Abraham's heart and saw a true commitment to do His will. Abraham believed that if God could send him a son when he was 100 years old He could surely retrieve that son from death. As a result, God entrusted to Abraham His kingdom on earth.

6. Bondage Through Wealth

Financial bondage also can exist even with an abundance of money. Those who use their money for self-satisfaction or hoard it all for the elusive "rainy day" also are bound. The accumulation of wealth and the physical possession of money can become an obsession that will destroy health, family, and friends. Suddenly everything and everybody become objects to be used to make more money.

There are choices to be made. *Circle the ones below* that you will do; make your commitment public, especially husbands and wives; and then do it!

| Use people | Love things | Serve money |
| Use things | Love people | Serve God |

"If I have put my confidence in gold, and called fine gold my trust, if I have gloated because my wealth was great, and because my hand secured so much... That too would have been an iniquity calling for judgment, for I would have denied God above" **(Job 31:24–25, 28).**

What did Job say was the real danger in riches? _denying God_

_____

_____

2 This attitude is not confined to non-Christians. Many Christians fall into Satan's snare and convert the very resources God provided for their peace and comfort into something full of pain and sorrow.

Financial bondage can be caused by different things. Check any or all that may apply to you.

_____	poor planning
✓	poor financial habits *no budget*
_____	lack of discipline
_____	greed or impatience
_____	desire for status
✓	fear for the future
✓	lack of sound counsel
_____	ignorance of God's Word
_____	other _____

God does not condemn wealth. He condemns the misuse of wealth. Attitude is the key!

start

Conditions of Servitude

In order to find God's financial solutions, it is first necessary to recognize the problems. Too many times we treat symptoms rather than problems. As previously discussed, circumstances are merely consequences of earlier wrong attitudes. We want to treat the real issues—not just the symptoms. We want to be "cured," not just released from the "pain."

Christians can assess whether a problem attitude exists if any of the following symptoms apply.

1. Overdue Bills

Anxiety, frustration, and worry occur when bills cannot be paid.

> *"Do not withhold good from those to whom it is due, when it is in your power to do it. Do not say to your neighbor, 'Go, and come back, and tomorrow I will give it,' when you have it with you"* (Proverbs 3:27-28).

What does God's Word warn against? *not paying your bills*

2. Worry About Investments

Anyone overly concerned about retirement, savings, or anything else that distracts from God's will and service can become a servant to it.

> *"No one can serve two masters; for either he will hate the one and love the other, or he will be devoted to one and despise the other. You cannot serve God and wealth"* (Matthew 6:24).

God condemns *hording* of money, not its possession.

> *"What is a man profited if he gains the whole world, and loses or forfeits himself?"* (Luke 9:25).

What was Jesus' warning here? *Could have all possessions and loose your soul to hell*

3. A Get-Rich-Quick Attitude

Profit without effort is the attitude behind every get-rich-quick scheme. It is a something-for-nothing mentality.

> *"A faithful man will abound with blessings, but he who makes haste to be rich will not go unpunished"* (Proverbs 28:20).

There are two promises in this verse. Explain each in your own words.

a. The faithful *will be blessed by God*

b. The hasty *will be punished in some way*

> *"A man with an evil eye hastens after wealth and does not know that want will come upon him"* (Proverbs 28:22).

According to this verse, how is one who seeks quick riches described? *evil eye*

always unsatisfied

What is the ultimate outcome? *never satisfied*

4. Laziness

God specifically condemns slothfulness and has established guidelines for us to follow. He warns us about the result of this dangerous attitude.

> *"The desire of the sluggard puts him to death, for his hands refuse to work; all day long he is craving, while the righteous gives and does not hold back"* (Proverbs 21:25–26).

What do you think these verses mean? *the lazy always looks out after himself looking to get – righteous gives*

Sometimes lazy people depend on others to take care of their needs, which resulted from irresponsibility.

> *"Even when we were with you, we used to give you this order: if anyone is not willing to work, then he is not to eat, either"* (2 Thessalonians 3:10).

Describe the application of this verse in your own words. Remember, this means those who will not work—not those who cannot work.

everyone should work if possible

5. Deceitfulness

Deceitfulness refers not only to lying to others; it also is not being entirely honest. Many people today seem to believe that they cannot be both successful and honest. That is a lie promoted by Satan.

> *"Better is a poor man who walks in his integrity than he who is perverse in speech and is a fool"* (Proverbs 19:1).

A *lie* is equated to a *fool*.

Too many times we treat symptoms rather than problems.

"He who practices deceit shall not dwell within my house; he who speaks false-hood shall not maintain his position before me" (Psalm 101:7).

There are no white lies in God's evaluation. Explain this verse in your own words.

God hates lies and looks down on liers not allowing them in heaven because they need to believe the Truth.

6. Greediness

When we consistently crave more than we have or always demand the best, that is being greedy. Materialism becomes the object of our lives.

"The wicked boasts of his heart's desire, and the greedy man curses and spurns the Lord" (Psalm 10:3).

How is greed ultimately manifested? __curse and spurn the Lord__

"Beware, and be on your guard against every form of greed; for not even when one has an abundance does his life consist of his possessions" (Luke 12:15).

What is the point of this verse? Life is about more than our possessions so do not look always for more.

7. Covetousness

Desiring what someone else has is promoted by the advertising media as being acceptable and normal. However, God's Word describes this attitude differently.

"This you know with certainty, that no immoral or impure person or covetous man, who is an idolater, has an inheritance in the kingdom of Christ and God" (Ephesians 5:5).

What is the danger of being covetous? __no place in heaven__

"I wrote to you not to associate with any so-called brother if he is an immoral person, or covetous, or an idolater, or a reviler, or a drunkard, or a swindler—not even to eat with such a one" (1 Corinthians 5:11).

What is God's admonition in this verse? __Do not be influenced by evil.__

_____

_____

start

Supplemental Study

1. Family Needs Unmet

   Wasting money to the point that basic needs go unmet is common today.

   > *"If anyone does not provide for his own, and especially for those of his household, he has denied the faith and is worse than an unbeliever"* (1 Timothy 5:8).

   What did Jesus say you do when you don't take care of the needs of family?

   I have denied the faith and is worse than an unbeliever

Those who depend on riches to make them feel superior to others will eventually find out how poor they are.

2. Overcommitment

   When we reverse the order of priorities in our lives, we suffer both spiritually and financially. Overcommitment is as extreme as slothfulness.

   > *"It is vain for you to rise up early, to retire late, to eat the bread of painful labors; for He gives to His beloved even in his sleep"* (Psalm 127:2).

   Explain what you think this verse means.

   Need to rest

   _____

3. Self-Indulgence

   A self-first attitude normally is characterized by irresponsible spending for things that yield temporary satisfaction and little usefulness. One who is never willing to deny impulses to spend and constantly seeks to indulge whimsical desires will always be in spiritual and financial bondage.

   > *"The seed which fell among the thorns, these are the ones who have heard, and as they go on their way they are choked with worries and riches and pleasures of this life, and bring no fruit to maturity"* (Luke 8:14).

   In this verse, what three factors result in an unfruitful life?

   a. _worries_

   b. _riches_

   c. _pleasures of life (TV, etc)_

4. Assumed Superiority

We don't usually think of this as an example of financial bondage, but it certainly is. Those who depend on riches to make them feel superior to others will eventually find out how poor they really are.

> *"They will fling their silver into the streets and their gold will become an abhorrent thing; their silver and their gold will not be able to deliver them in the day of the wrath of the Lord. They cannot satisfy their appetite nor can they fill their stomachs, for their iniquity has become an occasion of stumbling"* (Ezekiel 7:19).

According to this verse, when does God's accountability take place? _____

day of the wrath of the Lord

> *"Instruct those who are rich in this present world not to be conceited or to fix their hope on the uncertainty of riches, but on God, who richly supplies us with all things to enjoy"* (1 Timothy 6:17).

God's warning is not against wealth but against what? _where they fix their hope_

5. Financial Resentment

Many people in financial difficulty blame everyone but themselves for their problems. They have never submitted to God's authority or yielded to His wisdom. Inwardly, they might even resent God. Again, attitude is the keynote in God's plan.

> *"As for me, my feet came close to stumbling, my steps had almost slipped. For I was envious of the arrogant as I saw the prosperity of the wicked"* (Psalm 73:2-3).

What is the warning in this verse? _not to be envious_

The Principle About Borrowing

Before leaving this study on financial bondage, let's examine God's attitude toward credit. What does God's Word have to say about credit, particularly the fact that it's too available? Since the mid-1970s, when this book was first published, many things have changed concerning our use of credit. This area of finances causes more chaos in

Christian families than any other. But as mentioned earlier, the principles from God's Word still apply.

We must examine credit from God's viewpoint. That means we must understand what responses on our part are acceptable to God. He will direct us individually to a specific response. What is acceptable for one of us may be wrong for others. God's will is found in His Word.

> *"The wicked borrows and does not pay back, but the righteous is gracious and gives"* (Psalm 37:21).

Borrowing is not wrong, <u>*not paying back*</u> is.

> *"Owe nothing to anyone except to love one another; for he who loves his neighbor has fulfilled the law"* (Romans 13:8).

Does this mean that borrowing is unscriptural? <u>*—love is shown in repaying. (?)*</u>

Read verse 7 and see if the principle becomes clear.

> *"Render to all what is due them: tax to whom tax is due; custom to whom custom; fear to whom fear; honor to whom honor"* (Romans 13:7).

Living Proof Testimony

A woman, whose marriage was destroyed because of bad financial decisions that resulted in financial bondage, encourages couples not to maintain separate accounts and to communicate about all financial issues and decisions. She has learned how money can serve her rather than money being her master.

"My husband and I didn't talk about financial decisions. He paid some bills and I paid some. I resented the arrangement but he became angry when I raised the subject. We weren't saving, we argued all the time about money, and I was irresponsible about credit card debt. When we applied for a loan to remodel our home, my husband found out how much credit card debt I had. He lost it and he left us.

"I was in complete denial about my credit card debt but after he left I was forced to face up to my mistakes. I got on a budget, and I have paid off all credit cards except one. I pray that my husband and I can still work things out but he lost so much trust in me. Thankfully the Lord has given me strength to resist the credit card urges. I've come a long way but have a long way to go."

SESSION 4

RELEASE FROM SERVITUDE

"See to it that no one takes you captive through philosophy and empty deception, according to the tradition of men, according to the elementary principles of this world, rather than according to Christ" (Colossians 2:8).

RELEASE FROM SERVITUDE

Steps to Financial Freedom

The misuse of money causes frustration and worry, but God's plan provides peace and freedom. These qualities show themselves in every aspect of a Christian's life: the release from tension and anxiety about overdue bills, a clear conscience, and the sure knowledge that God is in control again. There's no guarantee that a Christian's life will be financially trouble-free; after all, we are human and we make mistakes. But once God is in charge of our finances, His divine correction will bring this area of our lives back under control.

There are basic steps to achieving God's plan. For every promise He makes, He has a prerequisite. In each case, some action is required to bring His power into focus in our lives. That might be prayer, fasting, or simply believing, but it will always require a free act of will.

Christians who are seeking God's best in their lives must be willing to submit to His will and direction. There are many Christians who say they trust God, but there is a big difference between saying and trusting. Some trust only when it's convenient to do so. Others trust only as a last resort. It all starts with a first step.

Contentment will come as a product of a relationship with God.

Balance is the key, as God's Word teaches.

Often wisdom is a result of learning what not to do.

God's plan provides peace and freedom.

Step 1. Transfer Ownership to God

There is no substitute for this step. If we believe that we are owners of possessions, then the ups and downs affecting those possessions will be reflected in our attitudes. However, if we have transferred all ownership to God, then God can move providentially to accomplish His will in our lives.

> *"The Lord by wisdom founded the earth, by understanding He established the heavens"* (Proverbs 3:19).

According to this verse, who is the real owner of everything?

The Lord

"Riches and honor are with me, enduring wealth and righteousness" (Proverbs 8:18).

What are the four blessings that come from trusting God?

riches, honor, enduring wealth and righteousness

Step 2. Get Out of Debt

From my understanding of the Scripture, *debt is a condition that exists when any of the following* circumstances are true.

- Past due money, goods, or services are owed to other people.

- The total of unsecured liabilities exceeds total assets (in other words, there is a negative balance).

- Financial pressures produce anxiety. (God will give a sense of peace when finances are managed according to His will.)

a. There are ways to get out of debt.

   (1) Stop overspending.

   (2) Start repaying what you owe.

   (3) Don't borrow more.

Remember, if you didn't get into debt in one month, you won't get out of debt in one month. The principle of this verse applies here.

> *"Better is a little with the fear of the Lord than great treasure and turmoil with it"* (Proverbs 15:16).

In other words, it is better to have _*little with fear of Lord*_

than to have _*great wealth with turmoil*_.

b. The way to stay out of debt is to accumulate some savings.

> *"There is precious treasure and oil in the dwelling of the wise, but a foolish man swallows it up"* (Proverbs 21:20).

So, be _*wise*_ not _*foolish*_.

Step 3. Accept God's Provision

Anxiety about investments and profits will disappear when Christians accept God's provision. We must believe that His wisdom is superior to ours and that He does care about all our needs.

> *"Do not worry then, saying, 'What will we eat?' or 'What will we drink?' or 'What will we wear for clothing?'"* (Matthew 6:31).

Define anxiety *worry or stress*

Define needs *food, clothing, drink*

Peace comes from accepting God's plan for your life and making the best of it. Accepting a bad situation that can be changed through diligence is called laziness.

Step 4. Refuse Quick Decisions

One of the identifying characteristics of a get-rich-quick scheme is pressure to make quick decisions based on incomplete information. Any solid business plan will stand up to examination. As God's stewards, we must take time to learn and understand.

> *"The plans of the diligent lead surely to advantage, but everyone who is hasty comes surely to poverty"* (Proverbs 21:5).

Advantage (profit) comes from *plans of diligent*

Losses (poverty) come from *hasty decisions*

Step 5. Excel in Work

It is impossible to be slothful if excellence is the minimum acceptable standard for work. Too often Christians feel they should be second best or purposely fail; and they label that humility. That is not God's plan. We must strive for excellence.

> *"Whoever speaks, is to do so as one who is speaking the utterances of God; whoever serves is to do so as one who is serving by the strength which God supplies; so that in all things God may be glorified through Jesus Christ, to whom belongs the glory and dominion forever and ever"* (1 Peter 4:11).

According to this verse, how should we perform? *as God would*

Why? *that God may be glorified*

4
SESSION

Balance is the key, as God's Word teaches.

Step 6. Confession–Restitution

God tells us to put the things of the past in the past. Often that requires first making restitution to those who have been wronged. The lessons learned and the blessings received will be worth the sacrifice or discomfort that comes from setting things right. Deceitfulness and dishonesty are abominations before God, and effort is required to escape those habit traps.

> *"Zaccheus stopped and said to the Lord, 'Behold, Lord, half of my possessions I will give to the poor, and if I have defrauded anyone of anything, I will give back four times as much'"* (Luke 19:8).

What principle did Zaccheus adopt? _give 4X back anything stole_

> *"Therefore if you are presenting your offering at the altar, and there remember that your brother has something against you, leave your offering there before the altar and go; first be reconciled to your brother, and then come and present your offering"* (Matthew 5:23–24).

What three things does Jesus say we must do if we have offended someone?

a. _leave offering_   b. _reconciled to brother_

c. _present offering_

Step 7. Contentment

Greediness and covetousness are results of being discontented. To overcome those attitudes, we must seek contentment in a moderate lifestyle. That may be difficult at first, because we tend to look at the circumstances instead of looking to God; but there never will be peace in finances otherwise. The secret of a happy (contented) life is learning how to deal with both the good times and the bad and, like the apostle Paul, knowing how to be content with either. Contentment will come as a product of a relationship with God.

> *"I have learned to be content in whatever circumstances I am. I know how to get along with humble means, and I also know how to live in prosperity; in any and every circumstance I have learned the secret of being filled and going hungry, both of having abundance and suffering need"* (Philippians 4:11-12).

What was Paul's philosophy about being contented?

a. _get along humble means   going hungry_ suffer need

b. _in prosperity   filled   abundance_

Release
from
Servitude

"We have brought nothing into this world, so we cannot take anything out of it either. And if we have food and covering, with these we shall be content" (1 Timothy 6:7-8).

What does Paul give as the means of being content? _food and covering_

Often wisdom is a result of learning what not to do.

Step 8. Balance Commitments

Any imbalance in a life leads to frustration and eventual problems. That is particularly true of both overwork and laziness. Many Christians sacrifice both their families and their personal relationships with Christ to spend more time at work or recreation. Balance is the key word, as God's Word teaches.

"Do not weary yourself to gain wealth, cease from your consideration of it. When you set your eyes on it, it is gone. For wealth certainly makes itself wings like an eagle that flies toward the heavens" (Proverbs 23:4–5).

What is the primary teaching of this verse? _don't worry about getting wealth_

And then there's the other extreme:

"He who tills his land will have plenty of bread, but he who pursues worthless things lacks sense" (Proverbs 12:11).

Name a few "worthless" things in our society. _TV_

_____

_____

_____

Step 9. Sacrifice Desires

God expects us to live less extravagantly and not be swayed by the foolish sensualism promoted by the mass media. We must establish a value system that doesn't include the *"I deserve it!"* mentality.

Solomon is considered the richest man who ever lived, as well as the wisest. Often, wisdom is a result of learning what not to do. He says this is how he acquired wisdom.

"All that my eyes desired I did not refuse them. I did not withhold my heart from any pleasure, for my heart was pleased because of all my labor and this was my reward for all my labor. Thus I considered all my activities which my hands had done and the labor which I had exerted, and behold all was vanity and striving after wind and there was no profit under the sun" (Ecclesiastes 2:10–11).

What was the result of Solomon's indulgence? ___*not profit*___

_____ and ___*vanity*___

Supplemental Study

1. Put Others First

    There is no better way to suppress feelings of superiority than to put others first. Those who are blessed with abundance must recognize that it is a gift.

    "Be of the same mind toward one another; do not be haughty in mind, but associate with the lowly. Do not be wise in your own estimation" (Romans 12:16).

    What are the four points made in this verse?

    a. *Treat everyone fairly*
    b. *Don't think I'm better than them*
    c. *Associate with lowly*
    d. *Don't think I'm wise*

    "Do nothing from selfishness or empty conceit, but with humility of mind regard one another as more important than yourselves; do not merely look out for your own personal interests, but also for the interests of others. Have this attitude in yourselves which was also in Christ Jesus" (Philippians 2:3–5).

    This is one of my favorite verses describing our relationships with one another.

    How are we to regard others? ___*more important than ourselves*___

    Why? ___*because that is how Christ lived.*___

2. Accept God's Provision

God never promised equality in provision. But He does promise our needs will be met (sometimes through the abundance of others); therefore, Christians have roles in God's plan and must be willing to accept God's provision without resentment.

> *"At this present time your abundance being a supply for their need, so that their abundance also may become a supply for your need, that there may be equality"* (**2 Corinthians 8:14**).

What does the verse say we should do with our abundance? *Supply*

another's need

Why? *for equality and so they will help you to your need.*

Living Proof Testimonies

This letter, a testimony to financial freedom, begins with, "Hurrah, we did it!" This couple attended CFC seminars and practiced what they had been taught. "Two happy individuals that are 100 percent debt free" sign the letter.

"I just wanted to thank you for your godly advice. Thanks a million. It was a long journey but well worth it. Now I can stay home and home school our five-year old. We can face [the year] 2000 debt free. Now I want God's discipline in all areas of my life. I need to lose weight and my husband needs to quit smoking cigars! I have new confidence that God will help us as we cooperate with Him."

*　　*　　*

A man writes about how God showed them how to be contented and live better on less money now than they had previously.

"I made some bad financial decisions right out of college. I had $20,000 in school debt, racked up more than $6,000 in credit card debt, and had motorcycle and car payments. If anything was left at the end of the month (there rarely was), God might get it.

"Praise God that He gave me a wife who had no debt and was wise with her money. I started listening to you on the radio and read a couple of your books. Within three years we were free of debt (except for our house) and my wife is able to stay at home with our two children.

SESSION

God's plan provides peace and freedom.

Release from Servitude

"Then God led us to become missionaries to the business community. When we came on staff my salary was cut by a third. But because of applying biblical principles of financial stewardship a few years ago, we were ready to make the adjustment to the pay cut. You know it's funny, but it seems like now we're doing better financially with less pay than we were a few years ago.

"Please keep telling Christians that debt can hinder their part in the spreading of God's kingdom."

SESSION 5

FINANCIAL PLANNING— GOD'S WAY
(Part One)

"The plans of the heart belong to man,
but the answer...is from the Lord"
(Proverbs 16:1).

FINANCIAL PLANNING – GOD'S WAY

What Is Planning?

Often Christians question whether they should do any planning. They ask, "Well, shouldn't a Christian depend totally on God?" The answer is yes, but that doesn't mean we are to sit at home waiting for God to deliver manna again! Although some may think so, this is not God's design.

> *"Know well the condition of your flocks, and pay attention to your herds; for riches are not forever, nor does a crown endure to all generations"* (**Proverbs 27:23-24**).

Throughout the Bible, we see leaders making plans and seeing them through for God's glory. Planning is an essential element for success in any financial program—but particularly so for Christians. God is an orderly provider and expects the same from us. As we read in Proverbs, there is wisdom in planning.

Debt equates to bondage and is the number one destroyer of marriages and families today.

> *"By wisdom a house is built, and by understanding it is established; and by knowledge the rooms are filled with all precious and pleasant riches"* (**Proverbs 24:3–4**).

Describe the three essential elements in good planning.

<u>Wisdom</u>   <u>Understanding</u> <u>Knowledge</u>

The first step is to plan to correctly assess the problem, which will require more than a onetime effort. Don't be too general, but also don't try to develop plans that are inflexible. Remember that a Christian's life is not all peace and joy.

Financial Planning— God's Way

"Consider it all joy, my brethren, when you encounter various trials, knowing that the testing of your faith produces endurance" (James 1:2–3).

Usually, this verse is discussed in terms of temptation or discouragement, but it also applies to sticking to your plans. Tell about a financial trial you have had in the last year.

Paying for Seth's college –

For plans to succeed, God's wisdom must be weighed before every decision. Remember,

"The unfolding of [God's] *words gives light; it gives understanding"* (Psalm 119:130).

Planning can be broken down into two basic areas: short-range plans and long-range plans.

What are short-range plans? Short-range plans are executed daily and include paying bills, buying groceries, saving for a vacation, saving for emergencies, or even paying taxes. Everyone needs to establish short-range plans. Failure to do so does not eliminate them; it simply results in anxiety, anger, and frustration.

Where do you start? With a simple but workable budget!

"For which one of you, when he wants to build a tower, does not first sit down and calculate the cost to see if he has enough to complete it?" (Luke 14:28).

According to this verse, the Lord wants us first to *calculate the cost*

The Christian home should be characterized by orderliness and excellence. Neither is possible without good communication and good planning. The following principles will help you establish useful and biblical plans. As you complete these exercises, think of how you can apply the principles in your home. In many instances the discussion questions will not have one absolute answer but are designed to bring out individual insights in a group discussion.

Six Steps to Short-Range Plans

1. Establish Written Plans and Goals

   A *written* goal helps by providing visible, objective, and measurable standards toward which to work. In the area of finances, that plan is called a budget.

   > *"Commit your works to the Lord and your plans will be established"* (Proverbs 16:3).

   What is the first step in biblically based planning?

   > *"The mind of man plans his way, but the Lord directs his step"* (Proverbs 16:9).

   This verse explains how that can be accomplished.

   What is your role? _plan our way_

   What is God's? _direct our steps_

2. Commit God's Portion First

   Although this principle is developed more fully in the unit on sharing, it is an essential element in any financial plan.

   > *"Honor the Lord from your wealth and from the first of all your produce; so your barns will be filled with plenty and your vats will overflow with new wine"* (Proverbs 3:9–10).

   What is the purpose of our giving? _honor the Lord from our wealth_

3. Control or Eliminate the Use of Credit

   In many families today, credit is out of control. Debt equates to bondage and is the number one destroyer of marriage and families today. Families in bondage must stop the misuse of credit to ever escape.

   > *"Better is a little with the fear of the Lord than great treasure and turmoil with it"* (Proverbs 15:16).

   Write this verse in your own words. _No debts but just living simply is better than lots of nice things mortgaged to the limit._

God has a plan for your life. Follow His plan—not your neighbor's.

4. Learn to Be Content

Many families in financial difficulty think that generating extra income, such as having the wife work, is the easiest and best way out of financial difficulties. That usually is not the case. Most problems are caused by overspending, not insufficient income. In fact, more income will sometimes make a situation worse. As the total level of spending increases, so does the use of credit. Generating more money, consolidating loans, even bankruptcies just treat the symptoms, not the problems.

There are basic steps to take.

a. Reduce expenses. This may mean eating out less, foregoing a vacation, selling a boat, or even sizing down your home. But if God's peace is your goal, it's worth it.

> *"He who loves pleasure will become a poor man; he who loves wine and oil will not become rich"* (Proverbs 21:17).

This verse talks about the dangers of self-indulgence. __✓__ true _____ false

b. Pray first and give God an opportunity. Before purchasing, we should give God an opportunity to provide the items. If our purchases are in God's will, He may sometimes manifest Himself in our finances by providing from totally unexpected sources. One of the greatest joys in a Christian's life is to experience God's love through His miraculous provision.

> *"Rest in the Lord and wait patiently for Him; do not fret because of him who prospers in his way, because of the man who carries out wicked schemes"* (Psalm 37:7).

What three things does this Psalm say to do?

(1) _Rest in the Lord_

(2) _Wait patiently for Him_

(3) _Do not fret because of others having more_

5. Set the Goals God Has for You

If you allow others to establish your priorities, plans, and goals, you are going to be frustrated and unhappy. Remember that God has a plan for your life. Follow His plan—not your neighbor's.

> *"'I know the plans that I have for you,' declares the Lord, 'plans for welfare and not for calamity to give you a future and a hope'"* (Jeremiah 29:11).

It has been said that "When Jesus is all you've got, Jesus is all you need." But finding contentment in Him does not come naturally, because the world claims that happiness can be found only by drinking the right soft drink or by wearing the right brand of sneakers! Not so! As soon as you get the "right one," a new one will appear.

"How blessed is the man who finds wisdom and the man who gains understanding. For her profit is better than the profit of silver and her gain better than fine gold" (Proverbs 3:13–14).

According to these verses, success is _finding wisdom and gaining understanding_ and _____.

"The Lord gives wisdom; from His mouth come knowledge and understanding" (Proverbs 2:6).

What is the source of wisdom? _The Lord_

Everyone has an opinion but not everyone is qualified to give advice.

6. Seek Good Christian Counsel

To receive help, we must be willing to ask for it. Many Christians are willing to help others but will never ask for help themselves. That is called pride. No one is without difficulties, and periodically each of us need counsel and advice. Many people refuse to seek counsel because they refuse to admit they have any problems. That's nonsense!

"Listen to counsel and accept discipline, that you may be wise the rest of your days" (Proverbs 19:20).

What are we directed to do? _Listen to counsel and accept discipline_

Often some of the best counsel available is a godly spouse. In a marriage each partner brings half the assets (and liabilities) to the relationship. To get a good balance in the area of finances, both must participate (talk and listen).

"For this reason a man shall leave his father and mother and shall be joined to his wife, and the two shall become one flesh" (Ephesians 5:31).

Describe God's plan for a married couple. They are to become _one flesh_

There is a difference between opinion and advice. Everyone has an opinion, but not everyone is qualified to give advice. If you need to have your appendix removed, and you can get an opinion from your neighbor or you can get advice from a doctor of internal medicine for twenty years, to whom should you listen?

"The overseer must be above reproach as God's steward, not self-willed, not quick-tempered, not addicted to wine, not pugnacious, not fond of sordid gain, but hospitable, loving what is good, sensible, just, devout, self-controlled, holding fast the faithful word which is in accordance with the teaching, so that he will be able both to exhort in sound doctrine and to refute those who contradict" (Titus 1:7–9).

List the qualities of a good counselor.

1 _Above reproach_ 2 _not self-willed_ 3 _not quick-tempered_

4 _not addicted to wine_ Not pugnacious "quarrelsome" 6 _not fond of sordid_

7 _hospitable_ 8 _loving what is good_ 9 _sensible_

just, devout, self-controlled, hold-fast to Word

Use these as a guide with all financial counselors.

Living Proof Testimony

This couple attended a "How to Manage Your Money" study in the mid-80s. They wrote to explain how the principles they learned about planning helped them get out of debt and achieve peace of mind through some difficult times.

"In 1994 my husband left commercial real estate sales and entered a new career field. We recalculated our budget to fit a lower income and adjust to living costs where we moved. Four years later my husband reentered the commercial real estate in another city where he had no contacts. We knew it would take 12 to 18 months for him to generate significant commissions. Because we have lived by our budget, we had an ample reserve account to survive, trusting the Lord to replenish our savings when it was needed.

"We thank Larry Burkett for all he has done for our marriage and our peace of mind as we live our lives following biblical principles [of budgeting and planning] *regarding how we spend our money.*

"We have also taught [using the How to Manage Your Money workbook] *and when we do, it just helps us to review and embrace the principles it sets forth."*

FINANCIAL PLANNING—
GOD'S WAY

(Part Two)

"By wisdom a house is built, and by understanding it is established; and by knowledge the rooms are filled with all precious and pleasant riches" (Proverbs 24:3-4).

FINANCIAL PLANNING – GOD'S WAY

Establishing Long-Range Goals

What are long-range goals? They are a composite of short-range plans linked back-to-back. Few people make any organized short-range plans; even fewer have long-range plans. It's said that people spend more time planning their summer vacations than they spend planning their retirement or their children's college education.

As we progress in our careers, our incomes tend to increase; but, so do our lifestyles. Without good short-term plans, as well as long-term goals, we simply increase our spending to consume most or all of it.

The purpose of all financial planning is to meet specific goals, such as education expenses, a debt-free home, retirement, and giving.

On the other hand, these goals/plans keep our natural hoarding tendencies in check so that if we're blessed with a surplus we will use it for God's glory and not for our own security.

Without any prearranged plan, wealthy Christians tend to buy too much insurance, accumulate "toys," and, all too often, leave too much to their children.

Long-range financial planning, God's way, will provide but not protect. It will ensure that your resources are assets, not liabilities.

God's desire is that we establish reasonable, maximum financial goals.

Three Steps to Establishing Long-Range Goals

1. A Written Plan Is Always Best

   To help in planning, there are questions in Session 12 of this book.

   > *"Which one of you, when he wants to build a tower, does not first sit down and calculate the cost to see if he has enough to complete it"* (Luke 14:28).

   What are we told to do? _Calculate the cost_

   Why? _to see if we have enough to complete it_

2. Establish Maximum Financial Goals

Often, we make money doing what we enjoy. But later the motive becomes to accumulate more money for security. Even though a few thousand dollars used to be enough, eventually a few million won't be. The key is to establish your goals before you make the money.

Rather than minimum goals, God's desire is that we establish reasonable, maximum financial goals and predetermine that we will not allow excessive accumulation, which would put His resources in storage rather than in circulation.

"Instruct them to do good, to be rich in good works, to be generous and ready to share, storing up for themselves the treasure of a good foundation for the future, so that they may take hold of that which is life indeed" (1 Timothy 6:18–19).

What does God instruct us to do in this Scripture passage?

a. _do good_

b. _be rich in good works_

c. _to be generous and ready to share_

Storing what? _treasure of a good foundation_

What is our promised reward? _life_

"Take care how you listen; for whoever has, to him more shall be given; and whoever does not have, even what he thinks he has shall be taken away from him" (Luke 8:18).

I believe this verse means that God blesses those who do not think that what they have is theirs alone. What do you think? _Same_

_____

_____

3. Establish a Long-Range Family Plan

Family goals are fundamental to future success. If they are accomplished according to God's principles, the rewards will pass from parents to children. But, unless we have sound financial plans and goals, how can we expect our children to become financially responsible?

It is vitally important that the whole family be made a part of God's sharing plan.

Husbands and wives should discuss this with each other and then with their children. Give your children the joy of seeing you share from your resources also. Learned early, these habits and attitudes will pay dividends in freedom from financial obsession and greed.

> *"Each man's work will become evident; for the day will show it because it is to be revealed with fire, and the fire itself will test the quality of each man's work"* (**1 Corinthians 3:13**).

This verse suggests that our motives will be tested by God.   true ✔   false _____

> *"A good man leaves an inheritance to his children's children, and the wealth of the sinner is stored up for the righteous"* (**Proverbs 13:22**).

What inheritance would you expect a godly grandparent to leave?

<u>"Godly heritage — bring that child to the Lord?</u>

Supplemental Study

1. A Family Living Plan

    If we never establish a spending plan for our families, others will. Family members need to know the boundaries within which they can operate, and failure to establish those limits will result in overspending and ultimate bondage.

    > *"Your adornment must not be merely external—braiding hair, and wearing gold jewelry, or putting on dresses; but let it be the hidden person of the heart, with the imperishable quality of a gentle and quiet spirit, which is precious in the sight of God"* (**1 Peter 3:3–4**).

    These verses show that God stresses what? <u>inner man —soul</u>
    <u>spirit</u>

    Does that mean that all adornment is wrong? <u>no</u>

    What is the required balance? <u>being as good on the inside as you are on the outside</u>

    Every family must recognize the difference between needs, wants, and desires in life.

    > *"The Gentiles eagerly seek all these things; for your heavenly Father knows that you need all these things"* (**Matthew 6:32**).

God recognizes our _*needs*_ and promises to supply them.

In your own words, define need. _____
food & drink to survive – place to live

In the following verses, identify three basic levels of expenditures: needs, wants, and desires.

> *"Godliness actually is a means of great gain when accompanied by* contentment. *For we have brought nothing into the world, so we cannot take anything out of it either. If we have food and covering, with these we shall be content"* (**1 Timothy 6:6–8**).

The apostle Paul says that godliness must be matched with _Contentment_

_____

> *"Do not love the world nor the things in the world. If anyone loves the world, the love of the Father is not in him. For all that is in the world, the lust of the flesh and the lust of the eyes and the boastful pride of life, is not from the Father, but is from the world"* (**1 John 2:15–16**).

These verses suggest that the imbalance (materially) is caused by

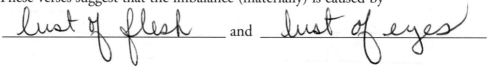 _lust of flesh_ and _lust of eyes_

The differences between needs, wants, and desires can be illustrated by the motives behind our buying.

- We all need clothing. The need may be satisfied by simple, basic garments—even thrift store bargains.

- Wants may be met by buying in an upscale, fashion-trend store.

- Desires may be met by buying exclusive, designer labels or custom-made clothing.

Every purchase should be evaluated and allowed or disallowed according to God's plan for your family.

Cindy

2. A Family Savings Plan

Many families fail to save and, consequently, are always in debt. Even minor financial setbacks plunge them into panic and anxiety.

"Go to the ant, O sluggard, observe her ways and be wise, which, having no chief, officer or ruler, prepares her food in the summer and gathers her provision in the harvest" (Proverbs 6:6-8).

What does the ant do? <u>*prepares her food in the summer*</u>

<u>Why?</u> <u>*so she can gather her provisions in the harvest*</u>

There is a difference between saving (for legitimate provision) and hoarding (for imagined protection). As we become wise stewards, we will learn to understand the difference.

God demands that we provide for our families; He doesn't say to protect them.

3. A Family Inheritance Plan

Consider the potential consequences of leaving large amounts of money to your family—either outright or in trust. Do you believe God will provide? Remember, God demands that we provide for our families; He doesn't say <u>to protect them.</u> Later we will discuss how much you can or should leave and how it should be evaluated in the light of God's plan—not the world's.

> *"He said to another, 'Follow me.' But he said, 'Lord, permit me first to go and bury my father.' But He said to him, 'Allow the dead to bury their own dead; but as for you, go and proclaim everywhere the kingdom of God.' Another also said, 'I will follow You, Lord; but first permit me to say good-bye to those at home.' But Jesus said to him, 'No one, after putting his hand to the plow and looking back, is fit for the kingdom of God'"* (Luke 9:59–62).

The first man was invited to follow Jesus, but he wanted to wait for his father's inheritance, which could be received only after the official burial.

Do you think the father's inheritance was a blessing or a curse? Why?

<u>*curse because he missed Jesus*</u>

> *"I have been young and now I am old, yet I have not seen the righteous forsaken or his descendants begging bread"* (Psalm 37:25).

In this verse, what is God's promise for descendants?

<u>*provided for*</u>

4. Establish a Long-Range Earning Plan

As mentioned previously, many people allow others to set their financial goals. Whether it's a hot tip on Internet stocks or a gold mine in the Yukon, if it's not in line with God's plans for you, you'll experience frustration, confusion, and loss, regardless of whether you make money or not. You should be sure your plans are in keeping with God's purposes. (As Will Rogers once observed, the problem with running in the rat race is that even if you win you're still a rat!)

"Do not be afraid when a man becomes rich, when the glory of his house is increased; for when he dies he will carry nothing away; his glory will not descend after him" (Psalm 49:16–17).

According to these verses, what's really important? _not riches but God_

"Make sure that your character is free from the love of money, being content with what you have; for He Himself has said, 'I will never desert you, nor will I ever forsake you' " (Hebrews 13:5).

We are to avoid _the love of money_
and learn to _be content with what I have_

5. Establish a Contingency (or Surplus) Plan

Once a limit on spending is established, most Christians can expect to accumulate a surplus. How that surplus is to be used must be predetermined or it will be diverted through lifestyle adjustments or hoarding.

With the best of intentions, many Christians hoard the Lord's surplus, much like the manna was hoarded in the wilderness.

God knows to whom He can entrust riches.

"His master said to him, 'Well done, good and faithful slave. You were faithful with a few things, I will put you in charge of many things; enter into the joy of your master'" (Matthew 25:23).

God is looking for a few _good_ and _faithful_
servants.

6. Establish Some Absolutes in Your Life

God will accept nothing less than complete honesty. Christians who are otherwise honest sometimes cheat when money is concerned—especially on taxes. To take every tax avoidance is both logical and legal, but to evade taxes is illegal and dishonest, and Christians must constantly be aware of the subtleties Satan will offer—all in the guise of shrewd opportunities.

> *"Because of this you also pay taxes, for rulers are servants of God, devoting themselves to this very thing. Render to all what is due them: tax to whom tax is due; custom to whom custom; fear to whom fear; honor to whom honor"* (**Romans 13:6–7**).

According to this verse, what are we to do? *render what is due because God allows gov.*

7. Husbands and Wives Must Plan

Most couples are opposites, and that's not by accident. We are attracted to people who complement us, not compete with us. If a husband and wife will accept God's wisdom in this and work together, they will accomplish much more than either can alone. God will not bless divisiveness. Read the following verses carefully.

> *"For this reason a man shall leave his father and his mother, and be joined to his wife; and they shall become one flesh"* (**Genesis 2:24**).

Husbands and wives become *one flesh*

Do you truly believe you are at one with your spouse? *yes most of the time*

> *"You husbands in the same way, live with your wives in an understanding way, as with someone weaker, since she is a woman; and show her honor as a fellow heir of the grace of life, so that your prayers will not be hindered"* (**1 Peter 3:7**).

Husbands are warned that *live with wife in understanding way*

if they treat their wives as *fellow heir of the grace of life*

> *"In the same way, you wives, be submissive to your own husbands so that even if any of them are disobedient to the word, they may be won without a word by the behavior of their wives"* (**1 Peter 3:1**).

Wives must be sure to *be submissive*

Special Assignment

As an employer:

> After praying about my work situation, I will do the following to improve relationships and productivity and thus help the business succeed.
>
> 1. _____
> 2. _____
> 3. _____

As an employee:

> There are several things I can do to improve my work, strengthen my testimony, and help my employer or supervisor succeed. To please God, I will do the following.
>
> 1. Quit complaining
> 2. Be satisfied with what I have
> 3. Take better care of my jeep.

Living Proof Testimony

A low-income family with four children says they have been on Larry's budget plan for nine years and find it outstanding. They see the practical value of long-range planning and setting goals to help them be prepared when unplanned emergencies arise.

"Recently my dryer has been causing trouble and my handyman husband is unable to fix it. However, thanks to our faithful God, planning, and your very practical budget, we are able to go out and hunt [for] a new dryer and pay cash for it.

"We even feel [good] about paying a little extra to get one that is a little better quality than average. Thank you for sharing the insight God has given you and making our lives a little better."

SESSION

MOTIVES FOR ACCUMULATING WEALTH

"All the ways of a man are clean in his own sight, but the Lord weighs the motives" (Proverbs 16:2).

MOTIVES FOR ACCUMULATING WEALTH

God's Attitude About Money

Now that we've reviewed what wealth is for Christians, we will examine why we should accumulate wealth. To accumulate means more than to store money. Accumulation refers to making, using, and spending money.

Money can yield comfort and convenience and can provide resources for spreading the Gospel of Jesus Christ. But money also can lead to covetousness and idolatry.

The love of money can ruin marriages, separate families, spoil children, and breed dishonesty. Therefore, it is vitally important to understand God's principles for accumulating wealth.

Giving is a ministry for many Christians. Once Christians accept giving as a ministry, a whole new area of God's Word becomes clear.

We must learn to understand the difference between opinion and counsel.

> *"Instruct them to do good, to be rich in good works, to be generous and ready to share"* **(1 Timothy 6:18).**

Along with the ability to make money comes the responsibility to share with others in need.

There are various motives for making and storing money; some are worldly, others are godly. List five reasons why you think people accumulate money.

1. security - fear of going without
2. comfort of nice things
3. greed - feel more important
4. selfishness - want lots of "toys"
5. to help others - go to college, be a missonary, etc

Tell what you believe is your primary motive for accumulating money.

help others — kid through college, church & mission help.

Why People Want to Accumulate Money

1. Some Are Advised To

Just as some people allow others to set their goals for them, other people allow friends, family, or society in general to define their financial priorities. Often they commit their lives to worldly success, to the exclusion of all else, including their relationship with God and their families.

> *"Without consultation, plans are frustrated, but with many counselors they succeed"* (Proverbs 15:22).

Why are we advised to seek counsel? *so our plans succeed.*

> *"The naive believes everything, but the sensible man considers his steps"* (Proverbs 14:15).

God says not to believe everything you hear. What does the sensible (knowledgeable) person do? *considers his steps or plans*

We should seek wise advice, but we must learn to understand the difference between opinion and counsel. No one else can make our decisions for us; the final decisions are our responsibility.

2. Some Accumulate Out of Envy

In Session 3, envy was identified as covetousness or greed. It is also known as social pressure or peer pressure.

> *"As for me, my feet came close to stumbling, my steps had almost slipped. For I was envious of the arrogant as I saw the prosperity of the wicked"* (Psalm 73:2–3).

According to this Scripture, what might happen? *you may slip in your walk with God.*

> *"Then He said to them, 'Beware, and be on your guard against every form*

of greed; for not even when one has an abundance does his life consist of his possessions'" (Luke 12:15).

What are we warned against? _think life consist of our possessions_

3. Some Make a Game of Accumulating Money

Have you ever known someone who was pursuing wealth like it was a contest or game? In those situations, everyone becomes a pawn–family, friends, fellow Christians. It's too bad that this attitude is promoted by elevating the "winners" to positions of spiritual leadership. In God's "game," if you compromise His rules, you lose!

"A good name is to be more desired than great wealth, favor is better than silver and gold" (Proverbs 22:1).

"What will it profit a man if he gains the whole world and forfeits his soul? Or what will a man give in exchange for his soul?" (Matthew 16:26).

Summarize the common theme in these verses. _To be liked and thought trustworthy and esp. to know God is mort important than any wealth or money_

4. Some Accumulate Money for Self-Esteem

This motive is particularly disastrous, because society promotes this weakness. We like to receive honor and recognition for what we accomplish. The accumulation of material things feeds egos. Even within Christian circles, there are those who want to be seen with only the "right" people. They use their resources to "purchase" esteem from everyone, including their families. They never give unless it is recognized and never share except to promote themselves.

"Instruct those who are rich in this present world not to be conceited or to fix their hope on the uncertainty of riches, but on God, who richly supplies us with all things to enjoy. Instruct them to do good, to be rich in good works, to be generous and ready to share" (1 Timothy 6:17–18).

a. What are the rich told to avoid? _being conceited or fix their hope on riches_

b. How is wealth described? _all things to enjoy_

Money is neither good nor bad, moral nor immoral. It is the use of it that will matter eternally.

c. Who is our only hope? _God_

> *"Pride goes before destruction, and a haughty spirit before stumbling"* (Proverbs 16:18).

What does pride ultimately lead to? _destruction_

_____

_____

Money is neither good nor bad, moral nor immoral. It is the use of it that will matter eternally.

5. Some Accumulate Money Because They Love Money

Those who hoard and store money because they love it usually won't part with it even for recognition and esteem. Their lives are usually characterized by stinginess. They may have accumulated thousands or even millions of dollars, but their loss of even a small portion is traumatic.

In Dickens' *A Christmas Carol*, Ebenezer Scrooge repented of his stinginess while he was still alive. In real life, others are not so fortunate. They will repent—when they stand before God. There is a sober warning:

> *"He will answer them, 'Truly I say to you, to the extent that you did not do it to one of the least of these, you did not do it to Me.' These will go away into eternal punishment, but the righteous into eternal life"* (Matthew 25:45-46).

Describe this warning in your own words. _hell or eternal_ _punishment_

_____

_____

> *"The love of money is a root of all sorts of evil, and some by longing for it have wandered away from the faith and pierced themselves with many griefs"* (1 Timothy 6:10).

What is the real danger of greed? _wander away from the faith_

_____

_____

6. Some Accumulate Money for Protection

Many people accumulate wealth for protection. Apparently they don't believe that God can supply their needs, so they hoard it out of fear.

At first the goal may be a few thousand, just to protect against future uncertainties. But to those who don't trust God, there never can be enough to protect against every calamity!

Again, there is nothing wrong with planning and saving–God's way. But people who hoard for protection only say they trust God. They don't really trust Him. In our society we are bombarded by ads for insurance of all kinds: life, health, disability, liability, calamity, and the like. Used in balance, these things are fine, but faith (trust) comes by hearing, and hearing by the Word of God (not by fear).

> *"Offer to God a sacrifice of thanksgiving and pay your vows to the Most High; call upon Me in the day of trouble; I shall rescue you, and you will honor Me"* (Psalm 50:14–15).

a. What should we do in our day of trouble? *Call on God*

_____

b. What is His promise? *He will rescue us and we will honor Him*

7. Some Accumulate to Supply a Spiritual Gift

There is only one reason God allows us to have a surplus above our own needs: to enable us to give. True wealth comes from the gift of giving. The interesting thing about God's plan is that when He finds a good steward who will share freely, He returns even more.

> *"Give, and it will be given to you. They will pour into your lap a good measure—pressed down, shaken together, and running over. For by your standard of measure it will be measured to you in return"* (Luke 6:38).

God says to *give* and it will be *given to us*

> *To those who don't trust God there never can be enough to protect against every calamity.*

The responsibilities of being wealthy are, in many ways, greater than those of being poor.

Motives for Accumulating Wealth

Living Proof Testimony

A couple, married for 20 years, is now enjoying a dream come true—the purchase of their first home with cash and a simple lifestyle of contentment. They have discovered God's attitude about money and have an alternative recommendation to "keeping up with the Joneses."

"I recommend shutting your eyes to the Joneses and instead, 'keeping up with God's principles.'

"After 20 years of low income, no financial help from family or government, not spending more than we made, and plain old contentment, we have a debt-free home. For 20 years we paid low rent (reduced by yard work and maintenance), and made simple, creative choices with food and clothing use.

"We also have a debt-free business (including a mortgage free building), and sons that are familiar with budget sheets, amortization schedules, accelerated principal payments (on our business property). . . and hearty leftovers.

"Our recommendation to folks is to adopt a contentment-based lifestyle, rather than simply looking for cost-cutting tricks that trim excessive spending."

HOW MUCH
IS ENOUGH?

"Beware, and be on your guard against every form of greed for not even when one has an abundance does his life consist of possessions" (Luke 12:15).

HOW MUCH IS ENOUGH?

Living Expenses, Investments, Retirement, Inheritances

Now that we have considered various motives for accumulating money, we can examine an important question: How much money is enough? Each of us is involved with making, spending, saving, and sharing the wealth God supplies. But how much should logically fit into each category?

How Much Is Enough for Current Provision?

Current needs means the total of your living expenses and your short-term cash reserves. It is not protection for the family (as we defined it in Session 6); nor is it the same for everyone. No two families will have the same goals within God's will or the same standard of living. In His infinite wisdom, God allows for many individual differences. But God's Word establishes some guidelines, and those guidelines should control lifestyles.

People who neglect to provide for their families are clearly outside of God's plan. Likewise, those who hoard and live lavishly are also outside of God's plan. It is easy to become entangled in a worldly lifestyle, but that lifestyle becomes surprisingly unfulfilling.

Christians who accumulate hoards of dollars ... will miss the opportunity of God's blessings.

During his lifetime, John D. Rockefeller was one of the world's wealthiest men. He was famous for tipping with shiny new dimes. When asked how much money he wanted, he always replied, "Just a little more." When he passed away, his accountant was asked how much money Mr. Rockefeller had left behind. His reply was, "All of it." Since this will be true for us as well, we need to ask, "How much is enough for my family?"

Balancing Work and Leisure

> *"I passed by the field of the sluggard and by the vineyard of the man lacking sense, and behold, it was completely overgrown with thistles; its surface was covered with nettles, and its stone wall was broken down. When I saw it, I reflected upon it; I looked, and received instruction. 'A little sleep, a little slumber, a little folding of the hands to rest,' then your poverty will come as a robber and your want like an armed man"* (**Proverbs 24:30–34**).

a. What does this proverb describe? _being lazy and having no sense_

b. What is the result of that characteristic? _overgrown fields that lead to poverty._

Contrast this with the following verse.

> *"He who tills his land will have plenty of bread, but he who pursues worthless things lacks sense"* (**Proverbs 12:11**).

c. According to this, what brings prosperity? _tilling the land or work_

Paul wrote to his disciple, Timothy, about keeping the right balance in his life.

> *"No soldier in active service entangles himself in the affairs of everyday life, so that he may please the one who enlisted him as a soldier"* (**2 Timothy 2:4**).

What are we to avoid? _~~entang~~ entanglements that affect our work_

But on the other hand, he sent a message to the lazy Christians in Thessalonica.

> *"If anyone is not willing to work, then he is not to eat, either"* (**2 Thessalonians 3:10**).

In other words, if you don't _work_ you don't _eat_.

I believe that reaching a balance in personal spending today is very difficult. We don't live in Africa or India. We live in the midst of overwhelming affluence: families have two (or more) cars, multiple television sets, stereos, computers, and designer clothing.

Deciding how to find that balance cannot be done without prayer and sacrifice. Solomon struggled with this when he wrote the following.

> *"He who loves money will not be satisfied with money, nor he who loves abundance with its income. This too is vanity"* (**Ecclesiastes 5:10**).

The danger is not money. It is _not being satisfied_.

Then Solomon wrote,

> *"The conclusion, when all has been heard, is: fear God and keep His commandments, because this applies to every person. For God will bring every act to judgment, everything which is hidden, whether it is good or evil"* (Ecclesiastes 12:13-14).

What two things did he advise? *fear God and keep His commandments*

and_____

Your plans should be compatible with God's purpose for your life, regardless of age.

How Much Is Enough for Investments?

Naturally, if a part of your ministry is the ability to make money and give it, you need an investment reserve. You should retain funds out of each investment to make additional investments. Unfortunately, too many people believe that amount is 100 percent. They take 100 percent of the proceeds of the first investment and put it into a new investment. Sometimes that is done for tax advantages to defer income, but it is not scriptural. God is capable of using His money in His ministry today. Many investors will be disappointed when, after having kept the Lord's money for years and never grasping the opportunity to share in His work, they stand before the Lord empty-handed.

Remember the parable of the servants? Review Luke 19:11-26. Several principles are presented.

a. The servants were given the same amounts.   true _____ false ✓

b. God expected them to invest His money.   true ✓ false _____

c. He expected the return of most or all of the proceeds. true ✓ false _____

d. The last servant was expected to double his investment. true _____ false ✓

When we invest with the wrong attitude, the same investments can be a source of greed, ego, and loss. The following are suggestions for investing.

- Choose wisely. Learn what you need to know before investing anything.

- Never risk borrowed money or money that would be hard to replace.

- Buy assets with utility (useful and multipurpose).

- Seek godly counsel from knowledgeable sources. Don't settle for opinions.

- Ask the Lord. Then wait on His reply instead of rushing ahead.

- If you don't receive God's peace in your decision, stop.

How Much Is Enough for Retirement?

Many people think they will need more money in retirement than they do during their working careers. That's not true. Once we've set a godly pattern for living during our lives, it shouldn't change after retirement, except to decrease in some instances. Even that isn't a great change in most cases. Christians who accumulate hoards of dollars to live a life of ease in retirement miss the opportunity of God's blessings during their more active years.

Actually, retirement as we know it is a relatively new innovation. Two or three generations ago, few people believed it was necessary (or possible) to stop being productive simply because they had reached 62 or 65 years of age. That same philosophy may be prevalent again as our society continues to age. That doesn't mean that you shouldn't plan toward a less productive period in the latter stages of life, but it does mean that your plans should be compatible with God's purpose for your life, regardless of age.

1. God speaks about fulfillment throughout a lifetime.

> *"Furthermore, as for every man to whom God has given riches and wealth, He has also empowered him to eat from them and to receive his reward and rejoice in his labor; this is the gift of God. For he will not often consider the years of his life, because God keeps him occupied with the gladness of his heart"* (Ecclesiastes 5:19–20).

a. Riches and wealth are described as _the gift of God_
(able to eat, receive a reward and rejoice in labor)

b. God says that age is a curse.   true ____ false _✓_

c. How is age described? _not considered because keeps us occupied with gladness of heart._

2. My Heavenly Father is aware of my needs.

> *"For all these things the nations of the world eagerly seek; but your Father knows that you need these things. But seek His kingdom, and these things will be added to you"* (Luke 12:30-31).

a. What is God's promise? _all things you need_

b. What does He require? _seek His kingdom_

How Much Is Enough for Inheritance?

Our society's preoccupation with materialism is abundantly reflected in this area. Christians who do not consider the consequences of large amounts of money in the hands of immature or irresponsible family members often leave them large sums in assets and insurance. We somehow believe that money provides protection, so we develop great "walled islands" to guard our loved ones.

But the story of the prodigal son shows the dangers of providing in excess.

> *"A man had two sons. The younger of them said to his father, 'Father, give me the share of the estate that falls to me.' So he divided his wealth between them. And not many days later, the younger son gathered everything together and went on a journey into a distant country, and there he squandered his estate with loose living.*
>
> *"Now when he had spent everything, a severe famine occurred in that country, and he began to be impoverished. So he went and hired himself out to one of the citizens of that country, and he sent him into his fields to feed swine. . . . But when he came to his senses, he said, 'How many of my father's hired men have more than enough bread, but I am dying here with hunger!' . . . So he got up and came to his father.*
>
> *"While he was still a long way off, his father saw him and felt compassion for him, and ran and embraced him and kissed him. And the son said to him, 'Father, I have sinned against heaven and in your sight; I am no longer worthy to be called your son.'*
>
> *"But the father said to his slaves, 'Quickly bring out the best robe and put it on him, and put a ring on his hand and sandals on his feet; and bring the fattened calf, kill it, and let us eat and celebrate; for this son of mine was dead and has come to life again; he was lost and has been found.' And they began to celebrate"* (Luke 15:11-24).

The son had not learned how to earn or handle money, and so he wasted his inheritance. At least, in this instance, the loving father was still alive when his foolish son was ready to accept his counsel.

Paul expresses the joy of earning one's own way.

> *"I have coveted no one's silver or gold or clothes. You yourselves know that these hands ministered to my own needs and to the men who were with me. In everything I showed you that by working hard in this manner you must help the weak and remember the words of the Lord Jesus, that He Himself said, 'It is more blessed to give than to receive'"* (Acts 20:33–35).

1. In light of Paul's message, answer the following.

  a. Have you trained your children to manage money properly?

  working on it

b. Have you equipped them to earn their own way? *trying by sending to college*

c. Have you trained them to become givers rather than takers?
Still working on that

2. The following verse describes a husband and father who became a burden to his family.

> *"If a man fathers a hundred children and lives many years, however many they be, but his <u>soul is not satisfied with good things</u> and he does not even have a proper burial, then I say, 'Better the miscarriage than he' "* (Ecclesiastes 6:3).

What is the man's error? _____

_____

3. The apostle Paul wrote about providing for our families.

> *"If anyone does not provide for his own, and especially for those of his household, he has denied the faith and is worse than an unbeliever"* (1 Timothy 5:8).

Paul's assessment is that one who does not provide for the family has _____ *denied the faith* .

4. Fill in the blanks in this verse.

> *"A good man leaves an _____ to his children's _____, and the wealth of the sinner is stored up for _____"* (Proverbs 13:22).

This implies an inheritance of lasting, spiritual values as well as financial provision. The way this is accomplished is with an investment of time.

5. Finally, the Bible speaks to the vanity of storing riches without purpose.

> *"Then I looked again at vanity under the sun. There was a certain man without a dependent, having neither a son nor a brother, yet there was no end to all his labor. Indeed, his eyes were not satisfied with riches and he never asked, 'And*

for whom am I laboring and depriving myself of pleasure?' This too is vanity and it is a grievous task" (Ecclesiastes 4:7–8).

This assessment also could apply to hoarding riches for a family as well. We are guardians of our families. We nurture and provide for them, but if we attempt to protect them from the testing and character building that will bring them to maturity in Christ, we do them great disservice.

The question of "How much is enough?" is less concerned with how much you keep for your purposes than with how much you surrender to His purpose.

Living Proof Testimonies

This couple finds CFC's budgeting guidelines practical and easy to follow. They have discovered the ability to breathe financially. They have determined just how much is enough for them and, in just four years, have found "safety and peace" by living within their income.

"We truly appreciate the safety and peace that living within our means has provided. God has always been faithful to meet our needs and even some of our wants. It has helped us to be better stewards of all that God has given to us."

*   *   *

Missionaries, who met in college and went overseas on mission internships, returned stateside and were married. They quickly learned the benefit of living within their means.

"We were convinced by your radio program to live within our means and pay off our debts as soon as possible. This is exactly what we did by the grace of God. We both worked and I used my minimal income as a church school custodian to live on, while putting my wife's entire nursing income toward paying off our school loans.

"We were so excited to send our final loan payment. By God's grace we were able to pay off $30,000 in school loans in less than two years. We rejoice that we are now debt free and I can begin seminary. Our goal is to complete seminary with no more loans so we can be on the mission field as soon as God would have us there. Living on my wife's income while I attend seminary full-time will be a challenge, yet we believe God will provide for us all the way.

How Much Is Enough?

SHARING BY GOD'S PLAN

"Sell your possessions and give to charity.... For where your treasure is, there your heart will be also" (Luke 12:33-34).

SHARING BY GOD'S PLAN

The Tithe—Is It Applicable?

This section addresses the scriptural principles of sharing according to God's Word. For spiritual growth it is essential to understand how important God considers sharing.

But first it is vital to accept the entire Bible as the inspired Word of God; therefore, the principles given in the Old Testament are as important as those in the New Testament.

> *"All Scripture is inspired by God and profitable for teaching, for reproof, for correction, for training in righteousness"* (2 Timothy 3:16).

Jesus taught regularly from the Old Testament and often amplified, but never refuted, the Scriptures. Rituals were clarified. For instance, it is no longer necessary to make blood sacrifices, because Jesus' blood was given as the ultimate sacrifice for sin. And we are no longer slaves to the law, because Christ's death has pardoned us. But, for a Christian who is actively seeking God's will, God's principles point the way to peace, happiness, and prosperity. The Creator of the Universe has promised to guide us in the management of our finances if we follow His principles.

The tithe... has always been an outside testimony of heart attitude.

There are scores of Scripture verses that relate to the reasons for sharing from what God supplies. Let's examine a few.

1. The Tithe

    The tithe is often misunderstood. Some Christians believe the tithe is a legalistic rule affecting only Old Testament Jews and has no real meaning today. Others believe tithing is a qualification for being a Christian and failure to tithe will result in God's expelling us from our relationship with Him. Neither is correct.

    The tithe—from its origin in the Old Testament—has always been an outside testimony of heart attitude.

"Melchizedek king of Salem brought out bread and wine; now he was a priest of God Most High. He blessed him and said, 'Blessed be Abram of God Most High, possessor of heaven and earth; and blessed be God Most High, Who has delivered your enemies into your hand.' He gave him a tenth of all" (Genesis 14:18–20).

a. What did Abram give to Melchizedek? _tenth of all he had_

"This Melchizedek. . . is king of peace. Without father, without mother, without genealogy, having neither beginning of days nor end of life, but made like the Son of God, he remains a priest perpetually. Now observe how great this man was to whom Abraham, the patriarch, gave a tenth of the choicest spoils.. . . But the one whose genealogy is not traced from them collected a tenth from Abraham and blessed the one who had the promises. But without any dispute the lesser is blessed by the greater. In this case mortal men receive tithes, but in that case one receives them, of whom it is witnessed that he lives on. And, so to speak, through Abraham even Levi, who received tithes, paid tithes, for he was still in the loins of his father when Melchizedek met him" (Hebrews 7:1–10).

b. How is Melchizedek identified? _as the Son of God_

c. Was Abraham obeying the Law of Moses? Yes _____ No _✓_

   Explain _Moses came after Abraham_

d. Why do you think Abraham tithed to Melchizedek?

   He was greater with power to bless

2. What the New Testament Says About Tithing

   "Woe to you, scribes and Pharisees, hypocrites! For you tithe mint and dill and cummin, and have neglected the weightier provisions of the law: justice and mercy and faithfulness; but these are the things you should have done without neglecting the others" (Matthew 23:23).

   a. Jesus reaffirmed the need to tithe, but He rebuked the leaders because they tithed legalistically.

"He who sows sparingly will also reap sparingly, and he who sows bountifully will also reap bountifully" (2 Corinthians 9:6).

What is the principle in this verse? *give generously and God will bless generously*

Does this mean that a Christian should tithe with a selfish motive? *no*

9
SESSION

He returns and multiplies to those who give freely and without looking for profit in their giving.

The following verse clears up any confusion.

> *"Who has first given to Him that it might be paid back to him again?"* (Romans 11:35).

So the principle is that the first part and the last part belong to God. He returns and multiplies to those who give freely and without looking for profit in their giving. God is under no obligation to multiply our gifts. He does so because He loves us.

Turning to the Old Testament, we can see that tithing simply reflects the heart attitude.

> *"Will a man rob God? Yet you are robbing Me! But you say, 'How have we robbed You?' In tithes and offerings"* (Malachi 3:8).

To what does God equate withholding the tithe? *robbing Him*

> *"Bring the whole tithe into the storehouse, . . . I will rebuke the devourer for you . . . ,' says the Lord of hosts"* (Malachi 3:10-11).

What does God promise in return for the right heart attitude?

Prevent pest from destroying crops and bless us so much that we will not have room for it

> *"You shall surely tithe all the produce from what you sow, which comes out of the field every year. You shall eat in the presence of the Lord your God, at the place where He chooses to establish His name, the tithe of your grain, your new wine, your oil, and the firstborn of your herd and your flock, so that you may learn to fear the Lord your God always"* (Deuteronomy 14:22–23). *(respect and reverence)*

The purpose of tithing is "so that you may learn to" *fear the Lord always*

"The fear of the Lord is the beginning of knowledge; fools despise wisdom and instruction" (Proverbs 1:7).

The fear of the Lord is *the beginning of knowledge*

The bottom line is, we give out of fear (awe, respect) of the Lord; thus, God gives us His wisdom.

Giving Above the Tithe

Sharing in Obedience

Once we understand that giving is our testimony to God's ownership, it opens a higher level of sharing: sharing offerings above the tithe out of obedience to God's Word.

Opportunities arise as God reveals needs around us, and we recognize a responsibility to meet them. As in most things, balance is the key to biblical giving. It's important to verify the needs are real and that your giving doesn't help to maintain bad habits. But, when in doubt it's better to help than to ignore the needs of others.

1. Giving is the evidence of our obedience.

> *"The King will say to those on His right, 'Come, you who are blessed of My Father, inherit the kingdom prepared for you from the foundation of the world. For I was hungry, and you gave Me something to eat; I was thirsty, and you gave Me something to drink; I was a stranger, and you invited Me in; naked, and you clothed Me; I was sick, and you visited Me; I was in prison, and you came to Me'"* (Matthew 25:34–36).

a. God promises that the blessed will *inherit the kingdom*

b. The blessed are described as those who did what? *helped those in need*

> *"If a brother or sister is without clothing and in need of daily food, and one of you says to them, 'Go in peace, be warmed and be filled,' and yet you do not give them what is necessary for their body, what use is that?"* (James 2:15–16).

a. What is the bottom line in these verses? *need to act for physical needs before witness*

2. Giving is the evidence of love.

> *"Little children, let us not love with word or with tongue, but in deed and truth. We will know by this that we are of the truth, and will assure our heart before Him"* (**1 John 3:18–19**).

We are to show our love by ____*deed*____ and ____*Truth*____

Sharing from Abundance

Sharing from abundance means that we have much and we choose to share rather than to store. Once we give, we find that we can't outgive God. Giving from our abundance is a demonstration that money is not our master.

Sharing from *abundance* is, spiritually speaking, the next step up in giving. Jesus warned of the dangers that come with riches. The rich can have great difficulty following God's path.

> *"Truly I say to you, it is hard for a rich man to enter the kingdom of heaven. Again I say to you, it is easier for a camel to go through the eye of a needle, than for a rich man to enter the kingdom of God"* (**Matthew 19:23–24**).

Money is a deterrent to following God's principles. True _____ False __✓__

Explain ____*Love of money is the deterrent*____

So, sharing out of abundance is practiced by those who are committed and recognize God's blessing and bounty in their lives.

> *"If the readiness is present, it is acceptable according to what a person has, not according to what he does not have. For this is not for the ease of others and for your affliction, but by way of equality—at this present time your abundance being a supply for their need, so that their abundance also may become a supply for your need, that there may be equality"* (**2 Corinthians 8:12–14**).

Does God require equality in material resources? ____*no*____

Explain ____*but help all those in need*____

Giving from our abundance is a demonstration that money is not our master.

Sharing Sacrificially

We hear stories of the sacrifices made by Christians in other parts of the world so the Gospel can move forward. Often this level of sacrificial giving is almost unknown among the church in America.

A sacrifice is simply a commitment to give to spread the Gospel, even if it requires giving up our own needs. Those who have never given sacrificially truly have missed one of the greatest blessings in this life.

> *"Just as you abound in everything, in faith and utterance and knowledge and in all earnestness and in the love we inspired in you, see that you abound in this gracious work also"* (**2 Corinthians 8:7**).

Paul described giving as _Abound in everything gracious work_

> *"I am not speaking this as a command, but as proving through the earnestness of others the sincerity of your love also. For you know the grace of our Lord Jesus Christ, that though He was rich, yet for your sake He became poor, so that you through His poverty might become rich"* (**2 Corinthians 8:8-9**).

Paul compares sacrificial giving to _being like through Jesus proving the earnestness of others the sincerity of our love_

Giving is not a command. It is the outside indicator of the inside spiritual condition.

Worldly motives have clouded our thinking and dulled our sensitivity. Often our level of commitment to our brothers and sisters in need is to provide them with a ride to the welfare office.

God's work should not be hindered because of a lack of funds. He will simply redistribute the necessary funds to Christians who are sincerely seeking His will and who will sacrifice personal luxuries for the needs of others.

Jesus used the example of a poor widow to demonstrate to His disciples that the amount we give is not important. It is the heart attitude that matters.

> *"He looked up and saw the rich putting their gifts into the treasury. And He saw a poor widow putting in two small copper coins. And He said, 'Truly I say to you, this poor widow put in more than all of them; for they all out of their surplus put into the offering; but she out of her poverty put in all that she had to live on'"* (**Luke 21:1–4**).

a. How does Jesus describe the amount given? _not important_

b. How did this compare with the giving by the rich? _she gave all she has but they gave out of their surplus_

c. Why? _because it was just surplus for them_

Supplemental Study

Sacrificial sharing pleases God.

> *"Do not neglect doing good and sharing, for with such sacrifices God is pleased"* (Hebrews 13:16).

a. What are we told not to neglect? _doing good and sharing_

b. Why? _because God is well pleased_

God's plan for sharing consists of:

- *Tithe*–A testimony to God's ownership

- *Obedience*–Helping the obvious needs around us

- *Abundance*–Giving from our surpluses

- *Sacrifice*–Yielding our wants and needs for others

Living Proof Testimony

A newlywed who recently graduated from college married a financially responsible man—"except when it came to tithing." She was "raised to give ten percent off the top [gross income] to God." Her husband felt that 10 percent of the net income was enough. They discovered that the tithe is not only applicable in their lives but tithing also provides unexpected blessings.

"I explained to God that I felt we should tithe the gross, but knew that He also wanted me to be submissive to my husband (Proverbs 21:9 and an article in CFC NL). I knew that God would have to take care of transforming my husband's heart.

"Then my husband noted low offerings in our church and decided we should be tithing on our gross income. Hallelujah! God is faithful. I only prayed. God did the rest.

"Your ministry has not only helped us to be better stewards of our finances, but also has kept peace in this precious marriage. At peace in Phoenix."

DECIDING WHO DESERVES HELP

"Beloved, you are acting faithfully in whatever you accomplish for the brethren.... You will do well to send them on their way in a manner worthy of God" (3 John 5-6).

DECIDING WHO DESERVES HELP

Giving to the Family

A good question to ask is, Who really deserves our help? Are there those we should not help? If we ask other people, we usually get a variety of opinions. If we rely totally upon emotions, we'll end up broke and in need of help for ourselves. Therefore, the ultimate source of wisdom has to be God's Word.

1. Some We Should Not Help

   Why would God specifically direct us not to help someone?

   a. God may be using material difficulties to direct someone—perhaps something that may bring them to Him or strengthen their spiritual lives. If we interfere, we may cause this person to miss God's best.

   b. Sometimes people just want to satisfy their wants or desires; usually, we are free to help but not required to. There are those who are living in rebellion to God, and the way God may choose to reach them is through financial crisis. To interfere is to risk God's wrath or at least His irritation.

Sometimes good stewardship requires that we discipline our own families financially.

> *"Even when we were with you, we used to give you this order: if anyone is not willing to work, then he is not to eat, either. For we hear that some among you are leading an undisciplined life, doing no work at all, but acting like busybodies"* (2 Thessalonians 3:10–11).

If someone refuses to work, how are we instructed to respond to him or her?

Not provide food for him or help him

In our society, a lot of need is caused by a get-rich-quick attitude.

"A man with an evil eye hastens after wealth and does not know that want will come upon him" (**Proverbs 28:22**).

Describe this verse in your own words. _Someone chasing wealth instead of God will have wants coming after him._

Sometimes good stewardship requires that we discipline our own families financially. All too often parents support unruly, undisciplined children–to their own hurt.

"A wise son accepts his father's discipline, but a scoffer does not listen to rebuke. Poverty and shame will come to him who neglects discipline" (**Proverbs 13:1, 18**).

A wise son _Accepts his father's discipline_ and ____poverty____ and ____Shame____ will come on the one _who neglects discipline_

2. Those We Should Help

In this age of political correctness and crumbling moral values, there has been an effort to redefine the word *family*. Some sociologists say it is any two or more people living in the same house. Other people say a family can even be one person living alone.

God's Word teaches that a family is more than just husband, wife, and children. It also refers to a complete group that includes mother, father, aunts, uncles, brothers, sisters, grandparents. All are potentially deserving of our help, if they are unable to meet their own needs, even with their best efforts.

"If anyone does not provide for his own, and especially for those of his household, he has denied the faith and is worse than an unbeliever" (**1 Timothy 5:8**).

We are instructed to _provide_, not profit and not protect.

Define, in your own words, the term *provide*. _____
Help when in need

"If any woman who is a believer has dependent widows, she must assist them and the church must not be burdened, so that it may assist those who are widows indeed" (**1 Timothy 5:16**).

a. The family, not the government, is the first line of defense for

dependent widows

b. Briefly scan 1 Timothy, chapter 5, and describe a widow.

over 60 married only once faithful to her husband, well thought of

"Whoever says to his father or mother, 'Whatever I have that would help you has been given to God,' he is not to honor his father or his mother. And by this you invalidated the word of God for the sake of your tradition" (**Matthew 15:5–6**).

a. Why did Jesus confront the Pharisees? *because they tell their parents that they can't help them because the money was already give to church*

b. Why did He think it was wrong? *Because they broke God's command to honor our parents in favor of man's rule to support the church*

Sharing with Others

It seems almost inconceivable that there are hungry Christians in the world today, but there are. In fact it has been estimated that there are more hungry Christians today than ever before in history. The worst witness we can have before the world is to ignore the needs of those in the body of Christ.

"Whoever has the world's goods, and sees his brother in need and closes his heart against him, how does the love of God abide in him? Little children, let us not love with word or with tongue, but in deed and truth" (**1 John 3:17–18**).

God's expectation is clear: If I have a surplus and fail to help a Christian in need, what is missing? *love of God*

The worst witness we can have before the world is to ignore the needs of those in the body of Christ.

"If a brother or sister is without clothing and in need of daily food, and one of you says to them, 'Go in peace, be warmed and be filled,' and yet you do not give them what is necessary for their body, what use is that?" (James 2:15–16).

"For just as the body without the spirit is dead, so also faith without works is dead" (James 2:26).

1. James says that ___*faith*___ without ___*works*___ is ___*dead*___.

"Who then is the faithful and sensible slave whom his master put in charge of his household to give them their food at the proper time? Blessed is that slave whom his master finds so doing when he comes. Truly I say to you that he will put him in charge of all his possessions" (Matthew 24:45–47).

2. Jesus describes the steward (slave) as ___*faithful*___ and
___*sensible*___. When will his reward be given?
___*When the Master returned*___

Remember, rewards in eternity last forever!

Sharing with the Shepherds

Many Christians somehow feel that the shepherds of our faith should live at a lower standard than anyone else, but that is contrary to what God's Word says. Spirituality is not proportional to poverty. In the following passage, the apostle Paul presents several relevant principles.

[**Paul wrote**] *"Who at any time serves as a soldier at his own expense? Who plants a vineyard, and does not eat the fruit of it? Or who tends a flock and does not use the milk of the flock? . . . It is written in the Law of Moses, 'You shall not muzzle the ox while he is threshing'"* (1 Corinthians 9:7,9).

Explain this principle in your own words. ___*Benefit from our work*___

1. Support Those Who Minister

   "Beloved, you are acting faithfully in whatever you accomplish for the brethren, and especially when they are strangers; and they have testified to your love before the church. You will do well to send them on their way in a manner worthy of God" (3 John 5–6).

   We support those who minister to us by ___*generous gift*___

2. Live by the Gospel

   "So also the Lord directed those who proclaim the gospel to get their living from the gospel" (1 Corinthians 9:14).

   To summarize this verse: Those who teach ___*should be paid and earn their living from preaching*___

   Those who are taught ___*should pay*___

Sharing with the Unsaved

It seems obvious that most Christians would recognize the need to help the body of Christ (although even those needs go unmet many times). But, using that logic, we easily could exclude the unsaved.

Why would God expect us to use His money to feed the unsaved? Many Christians today question whether we should feed them. God shows how important this is to Him by the sheer quantity of references in His Word.

   "Give to him who asks of you, and do not turn away from him who wants to borrow from you" (Matthew 5:42).

This verse should make us all think before turning away from "street people."

Sitting on the curb outside a fast-food restaurant, a shabbily dressed man asks passers-by for spare change in order to get something to eat. Is he an alcoholic who will take the money and go down the street for a bottle of cheap liquor? You don't know but you have a tendency to judge his motives. Should you tell him he's a bum and ought to get a job? Is he a "professional beggar"? How do you know if he is capable of working? Do you "pass by on the other side," or do you touch him in some positive way with the love of God?

Consider again a passage we reviewed earlier.

"Then they themselves also will answer, 'Lord, when did we see You hungry, or thirsty, or a stranger, or naked, or sick, or in prison, and did not take care of You?' Then He will answer them, 'Truly I say to you, to the extent that you did not do it to one of the least of these, you did not do it to Me'" **(Matthew 25:44–45).**

When you do something for the unsaved, who are you really doing it for?

_____*Jesus*_____

"Whoever in the name of a disciple gives to one of these little ones even a cup of cold water to drink, truly I say to you, he shall not lose his reward" **(Matthew 10:42).**

Attitude, not amount, reflects the heart.

Where Your Gifts Should Go

We must be sensitive to God's direction in our giving. He provides opportunities not only to give to the needs of the saints but also to invest tithes and offerings in His work. Unfortunately, most of us are besieged by charitable requests. Some are deserving, but many are hucksters: unfruitful or dishonest. We should balance compassion with good stewardship. There are some questions we should ask of any organization that solicits our help.

1. Is the organization communicating a message true to Scripture?

2. Are people responding positively to its work and message?

3. Is the organization seeking and accomplishing biblical goals?

4. Are the lives of its leaders consistent with biblical principles?

Discussion Points

"He who gives to the poor will never want, but he who shuts his eyes will have many curses" **(Proverbs 28:27).**

God makes two promises.

1. One who gives to the poor will _____*never want*_____

2. One who ignores others' needs will _many curses_

It is important that we acquire the proper perspective concerning with whom to share and when. After reviewing God's Word, the following is evident.

- We are required to share in needs–not wants or desires (Proverbs 16:26).

- We are to help those unable to provide for themselves (Luke 14:13,14).

- There is no way to outgive God. The more we are willing to share, the more God can entrust to us (Malachi 3:7-11).

We are to provide for the ministering brethren in a manner worthy of God.

We are to provide for the needs of fellow believers.

We are to supply the needs of the poor–saved or unsaved.

Living Proof Testimonies

This single parent hand-printed a four-page letter to testify of God's great faithfulness to His own. She and her children were abandoned by her husband but provided for by God. She works four different jobs: one full-time, one part-time, and two "on call." She lives on a budget and is determined to stay out of debt with an annual gross income of $18,500. She seems to have found a balanced approach to giving to her family.

"Matthew 6:33 has been my life verse and I've found that promise to be more important daily. ('But seek first the kingdom of God and His righteousness, and all these things shall be added to you.') Living as a low-income single parent is difficult, but God is an awesome God. I'm a witness to His faithfulness. Please continue to challenge churches in this area [of ministering to single parents]. *I appreciate your ministry."*

*   *   *

A woman wrote to tell how volunteer budget counselors from CFC probably saved her marriage and definitely saved her family from financial ruin. They have come from the brink of bankruptcy to be able to help others.

"We were both so grateful for the counseling help we received that we became facilitators for the video version as a special Sunday evening class at our church. Only four families attended, but one family made BIG changes.

"Recently my husband lost his job. [However it was] God, in His wisdom, who extricated my husband from a company he disliked and provided a new job with a company he respects, with an increase in salary. My husband then received a severance check from his former company, which arrived in God's perfect timing.

"We were able to help a relative in distress, and our tithe from that unexpected windfall has allowed us to give to several ministries. We will be sending you a measure of our thanks knowing that you will use it to help others like ourselves.

"Thank you again for being there when we were truly at the end of our rope. Yours in Christ."

MAKING FINANCIAL DECISIONS GOD'S WAY

*"Trust in the Lord with all your heart and do not lean on your own understanding.
In all your ways acknowledge Him, and He will make your paths straight"*
(Proverbs 3:5-6).

MAKING FINANCIAL DECISIONS GOD'S WAY

Financial Breathing

In this section we will consolidate some of the previous principles into a plan for financial breathing. That is, exhaling bad habits and inhaling good principles. God's plan is simple; if it were not, how would most of us ever apply it? The Holy Spirit simplifies it for us and empowers us to do it–when we allow Him to.

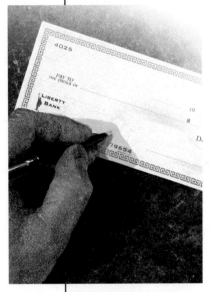

To put God's financial plan into action, we must do the following.

1. Acknowledge His Ownership Daily

   We must be certain that our daily decisions are surrendered to God. Just as challenges are a daily occurrence, so is the acknowledgment of God's authority.

   > *"So you will find favor and good repute in the sight of God and man. Trust in the Lord with all your heart and do not lean on your own understanding. In all your ways acknowledge Him, and He will make your paths straight"* **(Proverbs 3:4–6).**

Do we really believe God will do what is best, or do we just say we believe it?

To find favor with God and with others we need to:

a. T*rust* in the *Lord with all your heart*

b. Do not *lean on your own understanding*

c. In all decisions, *acknowledge Him* Him.

d. He promises to *make your paths straight*

> *"He was saying to them all, 'If anyone wishes to come after Me, he must deny himself, and take up his cross daily and follow Me' "* (Luke 9:23).

2. Accept God's Direction

Many times we ask God for direction but we precondition our requests with presumed answers. Do we really believe God will do what is best, or do we just say we believe it?

> *"If God so clothes the grass of the field, which is alive today and tomorrow is thrown into the furnace, will He not much more clothe you? You of little faith!"* (Matthew 6:30).

The prerequisite to receiving God's promises is _____. God promises to supply our needs even better than we would supply our own family's.

> *"If you then, being evil, know how to give good gifts to your children, how much more will your Father who is in heaven give what is good to those who ask Him!"* (Matthew 7:11).

In this verse God makes a promise, based on a condition.

a. What is the promise? _____

b. What is the requirement? _____

> *"Be anxious for nothing, but in everything by prayer and supplication with thanksgiving let your requests be made known to God"* (Philippians 4:6).

Anxiety has been described as an overwrought condition, brought on by fear of an event that has not yet occurred. God doesn't want us to be fearful and anxious.

We overcome anxiety by_____

_____

The following passage gives further instruction.

> *"Rejoice always; pray without ceasing; in everything give thanks; for this is God's will for you in Christ Jesus"* (1 Thessalonians 5:16–18).

3. Testify Outwardly of God's Ownership Inwardly

To breathe financially, it is important to establish a spiritual commitment to giving. Those who have experienced the richness of God's freedom know that surrendering the first part to God is an essential step.

> *"Give, and it will be given to you. They will pour into your lap a good measure—pressed down, shaken together, and running over. For by your standard of measure it will be measured to you in return"* (Luke 6:38).

a. God's instruction is to _____

_____

b. God's measure is _____

_____

We need to put the following principles into practice in our lives.

    1. Surrender all ownership to God daily.

    2. Accept God's answers.

    3. Acknowledge God's ownership.

Seek God's increase and avoid speculative schemes or unethical involvements.

Applying God's Wisdom

To live by God's plan, it helps to have a list of principles to consider in making decisions. We are all faced with numerous opportunities and choices that affect God's money. Left to our own logic and resources, we will usually miss God's best for us. By weighing every decision against God's principles, Satan's snares can be avoided.

Remember, these are *principles*, as opposed to laws. God has given them to enhance our lives because He understands what is best for us. Failure to follow His principles can result in both financial and spiritual loss.

The key point here is attitude. Describe in your own words the main theme presented.

_____

_____

_____

1. Avoid Hasty Speculation

   "Do not weary yourself to gain riches, cease from your consideration of it. When you set your eyes on it, it is gone. For wealth certainly makes itself wings, like an eagle that flies toward the heavens" (**Proverbs 23:4-5**).

We should seek God's increase and avoid speculative schemes or unethical involvements. Many times get-rich-quick schemes are not only unethical; they also may be illegal. The result of a Christian's involvement will be a loss of effective witness, a loss of money, and a loss of credibility.

Although there are many legitimate business opportunities, you should be particularly cautious when looking at unregistered stock investments, promotional land ventures, ground-floor startups, and any programs that promise quick, unreasonably large returns on your investment, particularly if they require you to make decisions before investigating the details and spending time in prayer.

2. Keep Your Finances Current

> *"Which one of you, when he wants to build a tower, does not first sit down and calculate the cost, to see if he has enough to complete it?"* (Luke 14:28).

The main theme of this verse is _____

_____

_____

It is never wise to buy beyond your means or do anything else that will jeopardize your financial freedom. Do not depend on some future event (such as a raise or potential sale) to meet obligations. Sacrifice wants and desires, if necessary, but stay within your means.

3. Do Not Go Into Debt to Do God's Work

> *"O fear the Lord, you His saints; for to those who fear Him there is no want"* (Psalm 34:9).

Although borrowing is not prohibited scripturally, not once in God's Word has He ever manifested Himself through a loan. This generation needs a positive witness of God's power and authority and it needs to start with Christians believing God in the area of finances.

The principle in the Psalm above is _____

_____

To launch out on "feeling" without clear direction and then realize that God's reputation will suffer if He doesn't provide the money is to test God and not trust Him.

An outright gift can be a testimony of commitment and ...provide an opportunity for sharing.

4. When in Doubt, Rather Than Lend, Give to the Needs of Others

> *"Because of the proof given by this ministry they will glorify God for your obedience to your confession of the Gospel of Christ, and for the liberality of your contribution to them and to all"* (2 Corinthians 9:13).

Although lending money to other Christians (without interest) is scripturally permissible, too often the result is a loss of friendship. When real need exists, an outright gift can be a testimony of commitment and will often provide an opportunity for sharing.

The principle of the verse above is that your giving gives the glory to

_____

5. Avoid Cosigning

> *"If you have become surety for your neighbor, have given a pledge for a stranger… do this then, my son, and deliver yourself; humble yourself, and importune your neighbor"* (Proverbs 6:1,3).

> *"A man lacking in sense pledges and become guarantor in the presence of his neighbor"* (Proverbs 17:18).

Scripture warns against cosigning wherever it speaks of "surety" (being liable for another's debts) and "striking hands" (making pledges, whether by contract or handshake). Cosigning is pledging assets against the debt of another.

By cosigning, you may encourage someone to borrow beyond his or her ability to repay. If someone values your friendship enough to ask for help, you may be able to help in other ways, including sound advice and creative solutions.

The principle expressed in the Proverbs above is a simple one. Don't

_____

6. Evaluate Purchases Based on Needs, Wants, Desires

"If we have food and covering, with these we shall be content" (1 Timothy 6:8).

God has promised to provide for our needs, but He has not promised the same for our wants or desires. Many Christians are unhappy because they can't discern the difference between needs, wants, and desires. We are told to learn to be satisfied with what we have.

The bottom line in Paul's letter to Timothy is _____

_____

7. Never Make Quick Financial Decisions

"Now for this very reason also, applying all diligence, in your faith supply moral excellence, and in your moral excellence, knowledge; and in your knowledge, self-control, and in your self-control, perseverance, and in your perseverance, godliness" (2 Peter 1:5–6).

The hallmark of most bad business decisions or purchases is the necessity for quick decisions. Almost without exception, pressured financial decisions are regretted later. Trust God's wisdom; if He is behind a transaction, there will be sufficient time to discern His direction.

The verse above addresses some essential characteristics of a Christian: moral

excellence,> _____> _____ _____,>

_____,> godliness.

God's perfect will may be served best by His saying "No" sometimes.

8. Accept God's "No" As Well As His "Yes"

> *"I know how to get along with humble means, and I also know how to live in prosperity; in any and every circumstance I have learned the secret of being filled and going hungry, both of having abundance and suffering need. I can do all things through Him who strengthens me"* **(Philippians 4:12-13).**

Remember that God's perfect will may be served best by His saying "No" sometimes. To the Christian who is trusting Christ moment by moment, quality of life is totally independent of circumstances. The ability to thank God in every circumstance demonstrates full dependence on Him, and God has often used financial matters to develop maturity in His children.

Summarize Philippians 4:13 and commit it to memory.

I can _____

9. If You Don't Have Peace, Don't Buy

> *"It is the blessing of the Lord that makes rich, and He adds no sorrow to it"* **(Proverbs 10:22).**

> *"Rest in the Lord and wait patiently for Him"* **(Psalm 37:7).**

Often we are not as responsive to God's guidance as we should be, because we become emotionally involved with an impending financial decision. As a last resort, God simply establishes within us a feeling of uneasiness to stop our direction. The principle to learn at these times: If you don't have peace, stop! Take time to pray and think about it; perhaps God has some alternative provision.

The key principle of Psalm 37:7 is _____

_____

10. Husbands and Wives Should Agree

God puts opposites together. In fact, it has been said that if the two of you are alike, one of you is unnecessary.

> *"The Lord God fashioned into a woman the rib which He had taken from the man, and brought her to the man. . . . For this reason a man shall leave his father and his mother, and be joined to his wife; and they shall become one flesh"* (Genesis 2:22,24).

God tells us that in marriage two become one (literally). Unfortunately, in practice many couples lead separate lives when it comes to finances. All too often the wife is strapped with the job of trying to balance unbalanced accounts and deal with hostile creditors, while her husband pretends to ignore the obvious. The end result is often hostility, remoteness, and nearly half the time the result is divorce.

Don't let this happen to your marriage. Face these decisions together. God will provide what you need. You must supply the discipline to live within those means.

> *"Two are better than one because they have a good return for their labor. For if either of them falls, the one will lift up his companion. But woe to the one who falls when there is not another to lift him up"* (Ecclesiastes 4:9-10).

11. Understand Who You Are

We are all uniquely different, but we also are similar in many ways.

If we are to get along with our spouses, it's probably a good idea to understand why we respond the way we do to financial situations, and it's critical to understand why our spouses respond the way they do.

For simplicity's sake, I will show the different personality styles in only four categories. Actually we are all blends of these styles, but usually one is distinct and dominant.

Take these assessments separately and then compare the results. You can get a good idea of why God put the two of you together. Each of you brings offsetting assets and liabilities to the marriage.

Remember two things: one, no personality is better than the other; two, these assessments are only guidelines, not absolutes.

Knowing who you are will help you to develop balanced, godly financial plans. God's best to you, and good planning.

By weighing every decision against God's principles, Satan's snares can be avoided.

Directing. If you are wired as a decision maker and a risk taker, you will tend to be much more comfortable in a new venture than someone with a low tolerance for risk. Perhaps God wants you to slow down and take the counsel of your more conservative spouse.

Interacting. If you are more easily swayed by the excitement of the crowd, you may tend to respond more to peer pressure than to a factual analysis. Perhaps God wants you to be less influenced by pressure from others.

Supportive. If you are steadfast and dislike change, you may tend to put off decisions rather than try something new. Perhaps God wants you to listen to your spouse, who is more flexible.

Conscientious. If you are a perfectionist and highly value precision, you probably tend to overdo everything. Perhaps God wants you to start without seeing the full picture, trust Him to lead as you walk by faith, and ease up just a bit.

Now go do it! Following Him in your financial and career decisions will always require more than a go-with-what-you-know approach or staying inside your comfort zone. But since you want to be a steward of God's resources, you must be willing to exhale your old habits and inhale good principles.

Christian Financial Concepts publishes materials to help you understand how your personality influences life choices, career, finances, and work habits. Our *Personality I.D.* program uses the DISC model of human behavior to help people understand the way they look at tasks and relationships. It is also available on CD-ROM. Our book, *Your Child Wonderfully Made*, shows how these personality traits help to form your child's outlook on life, work, education, money, prayer, relationships, and more.

Living Proof Testimony

A woman with more than $30,000 of credit card debt had difficulty making even minimum payments, and her stepfather bailed her out over and over. One day he told her it was the final time he would do so. She wishes he had refused to help her years ago. She suggests that what he did for her was a codependency issue; he was helping her stay in debt–not helping her get out. When he stopped enabling her overspending, she had to face the enormity of the debt. She found that following God's biblical financial principles provided much more than she expected.

"I had recently been listening to 'Money Matters' broadcasts, was convicted of my responsibilities, and began to repay my stepfather the $10,000 I owed him. I barely made ends meet but paid him little by little and repaid the credit card companies too. Truly the borrower is slave to the lender, and that's even when you have a merciful lender.

"I calculated that it would take me nine years to repay everyone. I determined that I would tithe and was even upset with God because I thought I could have paid the debt earlier using the tithe money.

"I guess this is a more testimony of the mercy and faithfulness of our heavenly Father to do what he knows is best whether we understand it or not.

"Two and a half years from the time I began to pay my stepfather back, God miraculously multiplied what I was paying and I paid back every dime. I am completely debt free and two years ago my stepfather helped me with the down payment on my townhouse. Only God's incredible grace could make such a change in me. PRAISE THE LORD!"

1. Score Your Surveys

a. Carefully separate the glued edges that attach pages S-1 and S-3. Then separate pages S-5 and S-7, if they were used.

b. Follow the instructions on the exposed pages and score the Person #1 Survey and the Person #2 Survey, if used.

c. Transfer your totals from the surveys to the spaces at the top of page S-9. You will use these numbers to plot your profiles.

2. Review the Example

a. Look over this example graph below to gain a general idea of what you will be doing next.

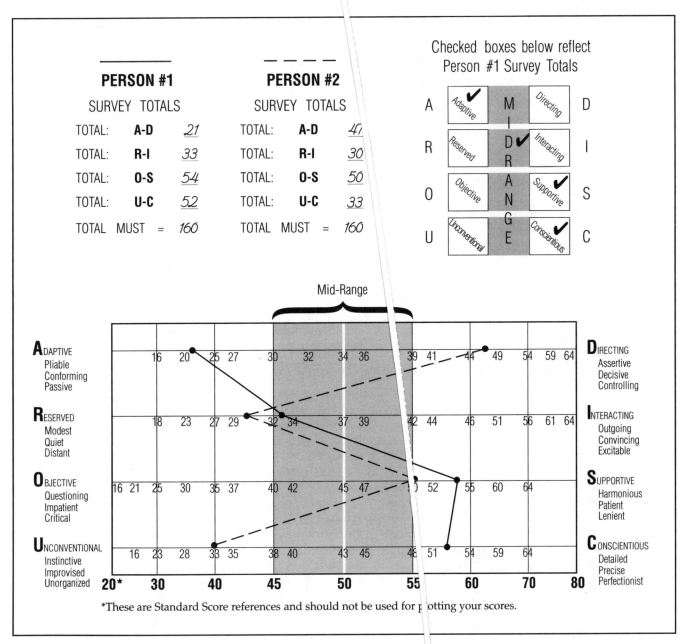

*These are Standard Score references and should not be used for plotting your scores.

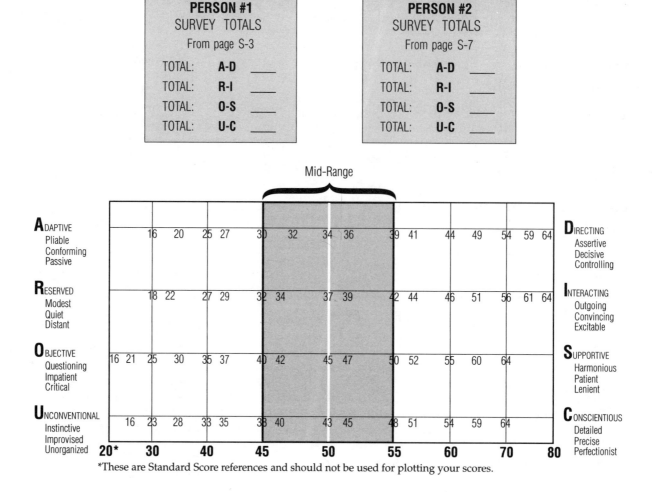

PERSON #1
SURVEY TOTALS
From page S-3

TOTAL: **A-D** ____
TOTAL: **R-I** ____
TOTAL: **O-S** ____
TOTAL: **U-C** ____

PERSON #2
SURVEY TOTALS
From page S-7

TOTAL: **A-D** ____
TOTAL: **R-I** ____
TOTAL: **O-S** ____
TOTAL: **U-C** ____

Mid-Range

ADAPTIVE
Pliable
Conforming
Passive

RESERVED
Modest
Quiet
Distant

OBJECTIVE
Questioning
Impatient
Critical

UNCONVENTIONAL
Instinctive
Improvised
Unorganized

DIRECTING
Assertive
Decisive
Controlling

INTERACTING
Outgoing
Convincing
Excitable

SUPPORTIVE
Harmonious
Patient
Lenient

CONSCIENTIOUS
Detailed
Precise
Perfectionist

*These are Standard Score references and should not be used for plotting your scores.

3. Plot Your Profiles

a. Using the totals from the Person #1 Survey, plot your AROU/DISC dimensions on the graph above; then connect the four points, using a straight edge. This graph reflects Person #1's natural personality profile. Refer to the example on page S-8 and note the solid line used.

b. If the Person #2 Survey is used, plot the points; then connect, using a dashed line or a different colored pen so you can easily see the differences between the two profiles.

4. Identify Your Natural Profiles

For each person, use the points on the graph above as a guide to **check the appropriate box at right to indicate his or her AROU/DISC ranges.**

5. Review Your Strengths and Weaknesses

The summaries on the next page indicate the strengths and weakness of each profile.

Person #1

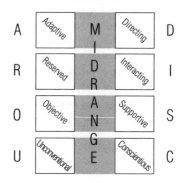

Person #2

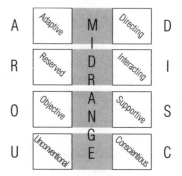

132

Typical Strengths and Weaknesses

The ADAPTIVE-DIRECTING dimension indicates the amount of control and decision-making authority desired.

Adaptive

STRENGTHS
1. Adapt to other's agenda
2. Cooperate
3. Move slowly into new areas
4. Be tactful
5. Focus on one thing at a time
6. Complete the current task

WEAKNESSES
1. Underestimate self
2. Not share opinions and judgments
3. Avoid taking charge
4. Not speak out
5. Be overly sensitive, internalize criticism
6. Lack assertiveness

Directing

STRENGTHS
1. Set the agenda
2. Compete
3. Move quickly to get results
4. Be bold
5. See the global perspective
6. Take on new challenges

WEAKNESSES
1. Be a poor listener
2. Be insensitive to others
3. Be impatient, critical
4. Tend to overcommit
5. Be demanding and pushy
6. Avoid routines and details

The RESERVED-INTERACTING dimension indicates the degree of social interaction desired.

Reserved

STRENGTHS
1. Works alone or one on one
2. Be serious
3. Be practical
4. Not worry about what others think
5. Be modest
6. Work quietly and listen

WEAKNESSES
1. Be withdrawn, alone
2. Appear secretive
3. Be pessimistic
4. Be curt
5. Appear shy
6. Drained by social contact

Interacting

STRENGTHS
1. Meet new people
2. Be enthusiastic
3. Be optimistic
4. Make a good impression
5. Be in the limelight
6. Be talkative

WEAKNESSES
1. Avoid working alone
2. Be uninhibited
3. Be overly confident
4. Need for approval
5. Be overly involved
6. Talk too much

The OBJECTIVE-SUPPORTIVE dimension indicates the degree of harmony/stability desired.

Objective

STRENGTHS
1. Use logic over feelings
2. Be tough-minded
3. Be independent and self-reliant
4. Manage conflict
5. Be eager
6. Be dynamic

WEAKNESSES
1. Be abrupt, restless
2. Be too critical
3. Be suspicious
4. Won't compromise
5. Don't finish projects
6. Be discontent

Supportive

STRENGTHS
1. Be empathetic
2. Be warm, compassionate
3. Be supportive
4. Promote harmony
5. Be patient
6. Be even-paced

WEAKNESSES
1. Be too sensitive
2. Be naive
3. Compromise too much
4. Be afraid to confront
5. Resist change
6. Be complacent

The UNCONVENTIONAL-CONSCIENTIOUS dimension indicates the degree of structure/detail desired.

Unconventional

STRENGTHS
1. Be spontaneous, unstructured
2. Be flexible, versatile
3. Be unconventional
4. Work with concepts and generalities
5. Rely on instincts
6. Take a risk

WEAKNESSES
1. Be unorganized
2. Be undisciplined
3. Be too informal
4. Overlook important details
5. Be overconfident
6. Be too reckless, careless

Conscientious

STRENGTHS
1. Be organized, structural
2. Be predictable
3. Be conventional
4. Work with specifics, details
5. Research for facts
6. Take a cautious approach

WEAKNESSES
1. Be too picky
2. Be inflexible
3. Depend on rules
4. Internalize emotions
5. Be a perfectionist
6. Be overly analytical

THE
CHALLENGE

*"A man shall leave his father and his mother, and be joined to his wife;
and they shall become one flesh"* (Genesis 2:24).

THE CHALLENGE

Congratulations! You are completing this study of the biblical principles of handling God's money. But with learning comes responsibility. You are now responsible to apply what you have learned in your family's finances.

To do that will require husbands and wives to work together, each using the abilities God has given. No financial plan will work with one person trying to budget and the other in opposition. Make a commitment to do God's work together.

If you're not married, find a friend who will help you be accountable. Usually the one who will help the most is the one who thinks the least like you.

Information without application is frustration.

1. Become a Steward

> *"He who is faithful in a very little thing is faithful also in much; and he who is unrighteous in a very little thing is unrighteous also in much"* **(Luke 16:10)**.

2. Give at Least a Tithe

> *"Honor the Lord from your wealth, and from the first of all your produce"* **(Proverbs 3:9)**.

3. Develop a Budget

> *"Know well the condition of your flocks, and pay attention to your herds; for riches are not forever, nor does a crown endure to all generations"* **(Proverbs 27:23–24)**.

4. Pay Off Consumer Debt

> *"The rich rules over the poor, and the borrower becomes the lender's slave"* **(Proverbs 22:7)**.

5. Become Debt Free

> *"It is the blessing of the Lord that makes rich, and He adds no sorrow to it"* **(Proverbs 10:22).**

6. Train Your Children

> *"Hear, my son, your father's instruction, and do not forsake your mother's teaching"* **(Proverbs 1:8).**

7. Teach Others

> *"The things which you have heard from me in the presence of many witnesses, entrust these to faithful men who will be able to teach others also"* **(2 Timothy 2:2).**

Note: The next step in this series is the *Family Financial Workbook* (Moody Press). Any good Christian bookstore will have copies.

Supplemental Information for Study
Practical Applications

Information without application is frustration. In this section you will find ideas to help you apply God's principles of finance. Each area should be prayerfully and carefully considered and then applied.

This section may be better used by filling out the plans as a family unit and then discussing the application in the group session.

Personal Communication Goals

Communication is vital to family financial planning. Questions are included for both husbands and wives, but it is best to complete them separately. Each should answer them on a separate sheet of paper as if the other spouse were asking each question. Then, without distractions, evaluate these together. Pray about them before you discuss your answers, and open your hearts to each other and to the Holy Spirit.

1. What are your personal goals for your life?_____

_____

_____

_____

_____

*A result of putting
Christ first in ...
marriage is not only
staying together but
growing together.*

2. What are your personal goals for the coming year? _____

_____

_____

_____

_____

3. How can I help you achieve your goals? _____

_____

_____

_____

_____

4. What can I do to help or improve our financial situation? _____

_____

_____

_____

_____

5. Do you think there's a proper balance between my outside activities and the time I

    spend at home? _____

_____

_____

6. Would you like me to do more around the house or do it differently?

_____

_____

_____

7. Among my activities outside the home, what do you think should be my priorities?

_____

_____

_____

_____

8. Do you think I should change anything about the way I dress, my appearance,

manner, or attitudes? _____

_____

_____

_____

_____

Other question: _____

_____

_____

_____

_____

Marriage Goals

A result of putting Christ first in marriage is not only staying together but growing together.

As a Christian couple begins to establish family goals, it is necessary to understand the roles each member satisfies in God's plan.

1. Do you believe our marriage is maturing and that we are becoming closer?

    _____

    _____

    _____

    _____

2. Do you believe we communicate clearly with each other?

    _____

    _____

    _____

    _____

3. Do you feel that I am sensitive to your personal needs? _____

    _____

    _____

    _____

    _____

4. What would you like me to say or do the next time you seem to be angry with me

    or are not speaking to me? _____

    _____

    _____

    _____

5. The next time you are late in getting ready to go someplace, what would you like me to say or do? _____

_____

_____

_____

6. What would you like me to do or say the next time you seem to be getting

impatient with something or someone? _____

_____

_____

_____

7. What would you like me to say or do if you begin to criticize someone?

_____

_____

_____

_____

8. Do you think I need to improve in getting ready on time or getting to meetings

on time? _____

_____

_____

_____

9. Should we go out together more often? _____

_____

_____

_____

10. Do I ever make cutting remarks about you or criticize you in front of other people?

_____

_____

_____

_____

11. What should I do in public to encourage you? in private? _____

_____

_____

_____

_____

12. Do I respond to your suggestions and ideas as if I had already thought of them instead of thanking you and encouraging you to contribute more?

_____

_____

_____

_____

13. Do I tell you enough about what I do every day?

_____

_____

_____

_____

14. What do I do that shows that I love you? _____

_____

_____

_____

_____

15. What do I do most often that angers you? disappoints you? _____

_____

_____

_____

_____

16. Do I convey my admiration and respect often enough? _____

_____

_____

_____

_____

17. Do you think that in front of other people we "play act" a happier marriage than

we have? _____

_____

_____

_____

_____

18. What do you think 1 Corinthians 7:3-7 means in relation to our marriage?

_____

_____

_____

_____

19. What are the responsibilities of a helpmate? _____

_____

_____

_____

_____

20. _____Do we give each other the same attention we did before we had children?

_____

_____

_____

_____

_____

Other question: _____

_____

_____

_____

_____

Family Goals

As a Christian couple begins to establish family goals, it is necessary to understand the roles each member satisfies in God's plan.

1. What are your family goals? _____

    _____

    _____

    _____

2. Do you think we are achieving them? _____

    _____

    _____

    _____

3. Fulfilling Responsibilities

    a. (Wife) What can I do to help you fulfill your responsibilities as spiritual leader

    of our family? _____

    _____

    _____

    _____

    b. (Husband) How can I better fulfill my responsibilities as spiritual leader of

    our family? _____

    _____

    _____

    _____

4. Do you believe we are meeting the spiritual needs of our family?

    _____

    _____

    _____

5. What kinds of family devotions should we have? _____

    _____

    _____

    _____

6. Do you feel we have a consistent prayer life together? _____

    _____

    _____

    _____

7. What are the responsibilities stated for the husband or wife in the following passages?

    1 Peter 3:1-2 _____

    _____

    Colossians 3:18-19 _____

    _____

    1 Timothy 2:11-15 _____

    _____

    1 Corinthians 11:3 _____

    _____

    Ephesians 5:17-33 _____

    _____

The Challenge

8. Do you think we are adequately involved in our local church? _____

_____

_____

_____

9. Do you believe we are meeting the basic needs of our family? _____

_____

_____

_____

10. Should we improve our eating habits? _____

_____

_____

_____

11. Should we get more exercise? _____

_____

_____

_____

12. Do we make good use of our time? _____

_____

   a. Do we watch too much TV? _____

_____

   b. Should we have more hobbies? _____

_____

   c. Should we read more? _____

13. Family Discipline

   a. How and when should we discipline our children? _____

   _____

   _____

   b. What do you think is the biblical viewpoint of discipline? _____

   _____

   _____

14. Briefly note the responsibilities of parents and their children in the following passages.

   Colossians 3:20-21 _____

   _____

   Hebrews 12:5-11 _____

   _____

   Proverbs 3:11-12 _____

   _____

   Ephesians 6:4 _____

   _____

15. What kind of instruction and training should we be giving our children in the home?

   _____

   _____

   _____

   _____

Family Financial Goals

By conservative estimates, at least 60 to 70 percent of the problems in a Christian home revolve around finances. Communication is the first step to finding God's cure.

1. Do you think I handle money properly? _____

_____

_____

_____

2. How could I better manage our money? _____

_____

_____

_____

3. Do you think I am any of the following?

   a. Too frugal? _____

   _____

   b. Too extravagant? _____

   _____

   c. About right? _____

   _____

   Why? _____

   _____

   _____

4. Do you think I accept financial responsibilities well? _____

_____

_____

_____

5. Do you think we communicate our financial goals well? _____

_____

_____

_____

6. What is your immediate financial goal? _____

_____

_____

_____

7. What is your primary goal for this year? _____

_____

8. What is your plan for our children's education? _____

_____

9. What is your retirement goal? _____

_____

10. What do you think about tithing?

    a. Is it necessary? _____

    b. Where should it go? _____

_____

11. How do you feel about giving in general? _____

_____

_____

12. Do you like the way we live? _____

_____

_____

13. What changes would you like to see? _____

_____

_____

_____

_____

Living Proof Testimony

This couple states the challenge they have accepted to be God's stewards and succinctly explains how they went about doing so. They see stewardship as the cornerstone principle of the Christian walk.

"We are writing to encourage you and give testimony of how the ministry of CFC has changed our lives and outlook.

"We were married in 1983 and saved by God's grace and mercy the next year. We both had student loans, credit card debt, and auto loans to repay. It was quite overwhelming. We thought our troubles would be over when my wife got a job. It relieved a great deal of financial pressure. However, we had no concept of stewardship and no discipline to overcome the bad habits we had developed.

"In 1986 we purchased a home with a mortgage, bought a new car with a loan, and cosigned for a car for a family member. In 1987, our child was stillborn and my wife stopped working. The financial pressure began to build again. That was when she began to hear you on the radio. You imparted the wisdom and hope we so desperately needed.

"We developed a spending plan and stuck to it. We completed your financial stewardship counselors training materials and trained a team of people in our church to counsel others.

"Nine years and three kids later we are completely debt free. We have an emergency fund equal to six months of our income. We began, and regularly add to, three college funds and give a substantial amount to God's work. We did it all on one income.

"During the course of our odyssey, we became persuaded that stewardship is the cornerstone principle of the Christian walk. We must properly view our bodies, our children, our time, and all our possessions through glasses of stewardship. We firmly believe that when a Christian grasps and applies the concept of stewardship, everything in life becomes more God-focused. It becomes imperative that one complies with the wishes and commands of the owner, and it is unthinkable for one to ignore or avoid contact with the owner.

"The verse that is our rallying cry is 'Do not be conformed to this world, but be transformed by the renewing of your mind' (Romans 12:2). That is, stop thinking like the world and you will stop acting like the world. Stop acting like the world and you will glorify God.

"We pray that God will continue to use you to transform the minds of His people and to conform them to the image of Christ."

Appendix

You'll Find Help in the Following Resources
Available from Christian Financial Concepts
(Note: Unless otherwise indicated, all items listed are books.)

Resources

ATTITUDES
Business by the Book
Crisis Control
How Much Is Enough?
How Much Is Enough? (video)
Investing for the Future
Using Your Money Wisely
The WORD on Finances (topically arranged Scriptures and commentary)

BORROWING AND DEBT
Bill Organizer (expanding file, audio)
Business by the Book
Complete Financial Guide for Young Couples
Debt-Free Living (with *SnapShot Gold*™ CD-ROM*)*
God's Principles for Operating a Business (audio)
Great Is Thy Faithfulness (devotional)
How to Manage Your Money Workbook
Investing for the Future
Money Management for College Students **Workbook**
Money Matters 2000 (software and manual)
SnapShot Gold™ CD-ROM (software)
The WORD on Finances (topically arranged Scriptures and commentary)
Using Your Money Wisely
Your Finances in Changing Times

Appendix

BUDGETING

Cash Organizer (spiral-bound envelope system)
How Much Is Enough?
How Much Is Enough? (video)
How to Manage Your Money Workbook
Money in Marriage (workbook, CD-ROM, audio)
Money Matters 2000 (software and manual)
Using Your Money Wisely
The WORD on Finances (topically arranged Scriptures and commentary)
Your Finances in Changing Times

BUYING AND SELLING

Business by the Book
Complete Financial Guide for Young Couples
Crisis Control
How Much Is Enough?
How Much Is Enough? (video)
How to Manage Your Money (audio)
Investing for the Future
Money in Marriage (workbook, CD-ROM, audio)
Money Matters 2000 (software and manual)
SnapShot Gold™ CD-ROM (software)
Using Your Money Wisely
The WORD on Finances (topically arranged Scriptures and commentary)

GAMES

Larry Burkett's Money Matters™, The Christian Financial Concepts board game (ages 10 to adult)
Money Matters for Kids board game (ages 5 to 10)
My Giving Bank (children's bank)

GIVING

Business by the Book
Great Is Thy Faithfulness (devotional book for 365 days)
How Much Is Enough?

How Much Is Enough? (video)
How to Manage Your Money Workbook (audio)
Money in Marriage (workbook, CD-ROM, audio)
Money Matters 2000 (software and manual)
Two Masters (video)
Using Your Money Wisely
Window of Wisdom™ CD-ROM Scripture (software)
The WORD on Finances (topically arranged Scriptures and commentary)
Your Child Wonderfully Made
Your Finances in Changing Times

HUSBAND'S AND WIFE'S RESPONSIBILITIES
Business by the Book
Career Direct—Occupational (adult guidance system, CD-ROM or paper)
Complete Financial Guide for Young Couples
Financial Planning Workshop (audio)
How Much Is Enough?
How Much Is Enough? (video)
Money in Marriage (workbook, CD ROM, audio)
Money Matters 2000 (software and manual)
Using Your Money Wisely
Two Masters (video)

INHERITANCE AND WILLS
Crisis Control
How to Manage Your Money Workbook
Using Your Money Wisely
Will Kit
The WORD on Finances (topically arranged Scriptures and commentary)
Your Finances in Changing Times

INVESTMENT AND SAVINGS
Crisis Control
Debt-Free Living (with *SnapShot Gold*™ CD-ROM)
How Much Is Enough?

How Much Is Enough? (video)
How to Manage Your Money (workbook, audio, or video)
Investing for the Future
Money Matters 2000 (software with manual)
Using Your Money Wisely
The WORD on Finances (topically arranged Scriptures and commentary)

LENDING

Business by the Book
Debt-Free Living
Using Your Money Wisely
The WORD on Finances (topically arranged Scriptures and commentary)

MONEY AND YOUTH

Business by the Book
Career Direct—Educational (student guidance system, CD-ROM or paper)
Cash Organizer (spiral-bound envelope system)
Complete Financial Guide for Young Couples
Consumer Books for College Students
    Buying Your First Car
    Getting Your First Credit Card
    Preparing for College
    Renting Your First Apartment
Crisis Control
Debt-Free Living (with *SnapShot Gold*™ CD-ROM)
50 Money Making Ideas for Kids
Financial Parenting
Get a Grip on Your Money (ages 16 to 21)
How Much Is Enough?
How Much Is Enough? (video)
How to Manage Your Money (workbook, audio, or video)
Making Ends Meet
Money in Marriage (workbook with CD-ROM, audio)
Money Management for College Students
Money Matters Family Night Tool Chest workbook
Money Matters for Teens workbook (ages 11-14)
Money Matters for Teens workbook (ages 15-18)

My Giving Bank (bank)

105 Questions Children Ask About Money Matters

Great Smoky Mountains Storybook Series (ages 5-10)

 A Different Kind of Party

 A Home for the Hamster

 Last Chance for Camp

 Sarah and the Art Contest

Surviving the Money Jungle

Using Your Money Wisely

What If I Owned Everything? (ages 3-8)

The WORD on Finances (topically arranged Scriptures and commentary)

RETIREMENT

Crisis Control

Debt-Free Living (with *SnapShot Gold*™ CD-ROM)

Financial Planning Workshop (audio)

Finding the Career That Fits You workbook

Great Is Thy Faithfulness (devotional for 365 days)

How Much Is Enough?

How Much Is Enough? (video)

How to Manage Your Money workbook (audio)

Investing for the Future

Money Matters 2000 (software and manual)

Using Your Money Wisely

SINGLES' FINANCES

Business by the Book

Career Direct—Educational (student guidance system, CD-ROM or paper)

Complete Financial Guide for Single Parents

Crisis Control

Debt-Free Living

Every Single Cent (singles without children)

Financial Guide for the Single Parent

Financial Guide for the Single Parent workbook

Great Is Thy Faithfulness (devotional for 365 days)

How Much Is Enough?

How Much Is Enough? (video)

How to Manage Your Money workbook (audio)
Investing for the Future
Making Ends Meet
Money Matters 2000 (software and manual)
Using Your Money Wisely
Window of Wisdom CD-ROM (software)
Women Leaving the Workplace

VOCATIONAL DECISIONS

Career Direct—Educational (student guidance system, CD-ROM or paper)
Career Direct—Occupational (adult guidance system, CD-ROM or paper)
Career Direct—YES!™ (Youth Exploration Survey--guidance system,
    paper format only)
Finding the Career That Fits You workbook
Guide to College Majors and Career Choices
The PathFinder
Personality I.D.® (adult DISC assessment—paper or
    Internet version—www.cfcministry.org)
Your Career in Changing Times
The WORD on Finances (topically arranged Scriptures and commentary)

OTHER BOOKS BY LARRY BURKETT
Great Is Thy Faithfulness (devotional book for 365 days)
Hope When It Hurts (about catastrophic illness)

Fiction: *The Illuminati*
        Solar Flare
        The THOR Conspiracy

For further information about any of these resources or others, contact
Christian Financial Concepts, PO Box 2377, Gainesville GA 30503-2377,
telephone (770) 534-1000 or (800) 722-1976 or visit us on the Web at
www.cfcministry.org.

How to Manage Your Money Benefits

Included with this *How to Manage Your Money Workbook* is Larry Burkett's Interactive CD-ROM software program containing the *Personality I.D.* assessment and *The WORD on Finances* Scripture database. Although you are not required to use this software as a part of the study, it is designed to be used as optional support to the lessons you complete in the workbook.

Personality I.D.

* Discover the strengths and weaknesses in your personality, and learn how to balance those areas in order to be a better financial steward. Clear, concise explanations and graphics make the results easy to understand.
* Find out how your personality is designed to complement the personality of your spouse.
* Identify answers to key questions concerning money. How does my personality affect my reactions towards money? What personality types tend to spend irresponsibly while others save, every penny?

The WORD on Finances

* Conveniently access every stewardship-related Scripture in the Bible!
* Scriptures (NASB Bible translation) are categorized in more than 70 topics, including Right Attitudes, Wrong Attitudes, Credit, Giving and Providing, God's Blessings and Curses. Investing, Work and Wages, Government, and more.
* As a FREE bonus, the KJV Bible translation is also included in its entirely as a handy reference tool.

Personality I.D. Installation Directions

To install the software:

* If you have not already done so, turn on your computer and load Windows.
* Place the CD in the CD-ROM drive.
* Click the Start button and choose Settings: Control Panel.
* In the Control Panel double-click on Add/Remove programs.
* Click the Install button.
* Follow the on-screen prompts through the rest of the installation process.

If you have any questions about setting up this software, do not hesitate to call Christian Financial Concepts' technical support department at 770-533-9610 between the hours of 8:30 A.M. and 4:30 P.M. EST. You also may e-mail tech support at techsupport@cfcministry.org or try our technical support on the Web at http://www.cfcministry.org

The WORD on Finances Installation Instructions

To install the software:

* If you have not already done so, turn on your computer and load Windows.
* Place the CD in the CD-ROM drive.
* Click the Start button and choose Settings: Control Panel.
* In the Control Panel double-click on Add/Remove programs.
* Click the Install button.
* Click the Next button.
* Click the Browse button.
* Double-click on the WoF folder.
* Locate the setup.exe file and double-click it.
* Click the Finish button.
* Follow the on-screen prompts through the rest of the installation process.

System Requirements

Windows 95/98 or higher, 32 MB RAM (minimum), in VGA 256 color or higher resolution video (SVGA recommended), 50MB free disk space, Mouse or compatible *pointing* device, 2X CD-ROM or faster (4X recommended), Windows compatible printer for printing reports, soundcard recommended for audio portions of the program.